JUSTICE
FOR THE
POOR

Books from Sojourners

*Rediscovering Values: On Wall Street, Main Street, and Your Street —
A Moral Compass for the New Economy,*
by Jim Wallis (2010)

*Strangers in the Land: A Six-Week Devotional Guide
on Immigration, the Church, and the Bible,*
by the editors of Sojourners magazine (2008)

*Hungry for Justice: A Six-Week Guide for Praying Daily,
Building Community, and Changing the World,*
by the editors of Sojourners magazine (2008)

*The Great Awakening: Reviving Faith and Politics
in a Post-Religious Right America,*
by Jim Wallis (2008)

Living God's Politics: The Companion Guide,
by Jim Wallis, Chuck Gutenson, and editors of Sojourners (2006)

*God's Politics: Why the Right Gets It Wrong and
the Left Doesn't Get It,* by Jim Wallis (2005)

Available at store.sojo.net

Love God.
Serve People.
Change the World.

PARTICIPANT'S GUIDE

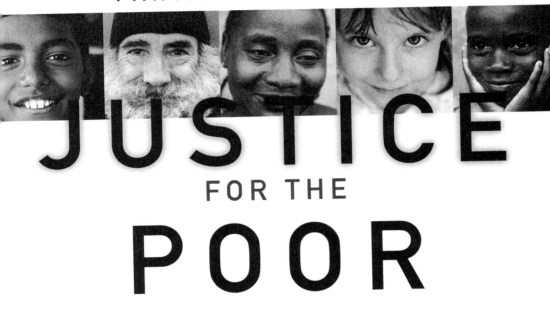

JUSTICE
FOR THE
POOR

Six Sessions

JIM WALLIS and SOJOURNERS

Written by Rose Marie Berger and Jeannie Choi

ZONDERVAN®   SOJOURNERS

ZONDERVAN.com/
AUTHORTRACKER
follow your favorite authors

ZONDERVAN

Justice for the Poor Participant's Guide
Copyright © 2010 by Sojourners

Requests for information should be addressed to:

Zondervan, *Grand Rapids, Michigan 49530*

ISBN 978-0-310-32787-5

Cover design: Rob Monacelli
Interior design: Sherri L. Hoffman

Printed in the United States of America

10 11 12 13 14 15 /DCI/ 25 24 23 22 21 20 19 18 17 16 15 14 13 12 11 10 9 8 7 6 5 4 3 2 1

CONTENTS

APPENDIX

I know that the LORD maintains the cause of the needy, and executes justice for the poor.

PSALM 140:12

INTRODUCTION

No more shall there be in it an infant that lives but a few days, or an old person who does not live out a lifetime.... They shall build houses and inhabit them; they shall plant vineyards and eat their fruit. They shall not build and another inhabit; they shall not plant and another eat; for like the days of a tree shall the days of my people be, and my chosen shall long enjoy the work of their hands. They shall not labor in vain, or bear children for calamity; for they shall be offspring blessed by the LORD.

ISAIAH 65:20 – 23

Any gospel that is not good news to poor people is simply not the gospel of Jesus Christ.

JIM WALLIS

Why is poverty and justice for those living in poverty important to Christians? When Jim Wallis and the founding members of the intentional Christian community called Sojourners were in seminary, they tried an experiment. They took an old Bible and cut out every single reference to the poor, the afflicted, the oppressed, those left out and left behind. They found several thousand verses in the Bible about the poor. In the Hebrew Bible, justice for the impoverished was the second most prominent theme; the first was idolatry, and the two were often connected. In the New Testament, one out of every sixteen verses was about the poor. In the three synoptic gospels (Matthew, Mark, and Luke), it was one out of every ten verses. In the gospel of Luke alone, one out of every seven verses was about the left out and left behind. When the young seminarians literally cut out all of these verses, the

Bible would no longer stay together. It was falling apart and in shreds, a Bible full of holes.

To understand the "poor" in the Bible as a reference to spiritual poverty only is to miss an important message. Indeed, faith without an understanding of justice for the poor is a gospel full of holes — incomplete and in tatters. Now, as in biblical times, financial poverty and spiritual poverty are related — but *not* in the way Christianized capitalism has told us the story. Material poverty does not occur because one is spiritually poor. Rather, in a society with extremes of wealth and poverty, a general spiritual poverty is experienced by all. When the wealthy are dying from diseases of overabundance and the poor are dying from inadequate health care, poor diets, and stress-related illnesses, the society as a whole is ailing spiritually as well as physically ... so how do Christians address poverty in *all* its forms?

Jim Wallis and the community at Sojourners ministries have been experimenting with this question while living in the Washington, D.C., neighborhood of Columbia Heights for more than thirty years. The neighborhood has seen its share of changes. When Sojourners moved there in the mid–1970s, it had a burned-out shell of a formerly thriving black business district. The 1968 riots that followed the assassination of Dr. Martin Luther King Jr. ran through the middle of Columbia Heights, and for nearly three decades the neighborhood was neglected. Poverty and violence were rampant, and the drug trade thrived. More recently, gentrification has brought Starbucks and Target to this once-forgotten corner of our nation's capital. It is from this social location that Sojourners reads the Bible and asks how it is "good news for the poor" today.

Justice for the Poor recaptures the spirit and power of the biblical vision that links poverty and justice for today's America. The Gospels give us insight about the poverty and political oppression that surrounded Jesus. He was born poor (Luke 2:6–7, 24), and his family became refugees from the violence of the empire when he was still a baby. His lifestyle was that of a "have-not" (Matthew 8:19–20). Jesus' teaching showed a tremendous concern for the masses (Matthew 9:36–37), which in Palestine were the poor. His stories about clothes that have to be patched, men who have to borrow a loaf of bread, and women who cannot afford to lose a coin show an awareness of poverty that is born of experience.

Through this study we will explore the experiences of people living in poverty in the United States today. How can we learn from those experiences? What are the responsibilities of Christians to prioritize the needs of the poor? What is the Christian call to advocate for changes in laws that affect the poor? By turning to the Bible for answers to these questions, our goal is to come away with a firm understanding of one of the major tenets of the gospel of Jesus Christ: justice for the poor.

"Burger King Mom": Being Poor in America

KEY ISSUE

The poorest of the poor are shut out of American life.

She was working at the drive-in window at the local Burger King, busy filling orders for Whoppers and fries and Cokes and large shakes. But whenever there was a lull, she'd go right to the corner table. Three kids sat there with books and papers and pencils out. They were doing their homework at four in the afternoon. And she was obviously their mom — likely a single mom, helping them with their homework between cars and customers. She's typical of many people in this country — often women with children — who are poor. She was invisible. You wouldn't notice her. And that's the problem.

Given her low wages, this single mother was no doubt balancing more than fast food and homework — perhaps deciding between paying the rent or buying winter boots for her kids. She has become an icon for the Sojourners community. We call her "Burger King Mom."

Why is Burger King Mom important to us as Christians? She exists in both the red and blue states, but neither party is much interested in her or her family's issues. She is part of the low-income demographic that is most unrepresented in American politics, with the lowest levels of both voter registration and turnout and a high percentage of immigrants.

Most Americans believe that if you work hard and full-time, you should not be poor. But the truth is that many working families are working full-time, and many low-income breadwinners must hold down multiple jobs just to survive. With stagnant wages in a difficult economy, more and more people and their children are simply being left out and left behind. When work no longer supports a family, the existence of a genuine "opportunity society" and the ethic of work itself are at risk.

The truth is that hungry people are going without food stamps, poor children are going without health care, elderly are going without medicine, and schoolchildren are going without textbooks because of war, tax cuts, and a lack of both attention and compassion from our political leaders. The poorest of the poor have been shut out of American life and our country has been divided into two separate and drastically unequal worlds: the affluent majority and the impoverished class; the "we" and the "they." In other parts of the world, the poor are even more desperate.

To be a Christian means to identify oneself with the good news that Jesus preached, namely, the gospel of the kingdom of God. Jesus' inaugural sermon in the little town of Nazareth made clear how, why, and to whom his message was such good news: "The Spirit of the Lord is upon me, because he has anointed me to bring good news to the poor. He has sent me to proclaim release to the captives and recovery of sight to the blind, to let the oppressed go free, to proclaim the year of the Lord's favor" (Luke 4:18–19).

One of the central themes in Scripture is the subject of wealth and poverty. It pervades the Hebrew Bible and the New Testament. The Bible is strong in its emphasis; the Scriptures are stunning in their clarity. As followers, we must reconnect with our original calling to bring good news to the poor. When we lose our proximity to and our relationships with poor people, we lose the essence of the gospel that Jesus preached.

As your group studies what the Bible says about poverty, keep these questions in the back of your mind: What do you think Jesus meant when he said that we will always have the poor with us? What happens when we put that claim in its broader biblical context? Why must Christians serve the poor? How can we restore the integrity of the Word of God in our lives through prioritizing the needs of the poor?

WELCOME (1 MIN.)

The Bible is filled with lessons on how people of faith should treat the poor — with compassion, mercy, and solidarity, for we all need the mercy of God as we live and work on this earth. In this session, through a study of Matthew 25, we see that God's heart is for the poor, the widow, and the orphan.

VIDEO TEACHING (20 MIN.)

Notes

Poverty and justice are important to Christians because ...

Matthew 25:31–46 is "good news" to ...

To be a true follower of Jesus, one must offer good news to the ...

When Christians lose proximity to and relationship with the poor, we lose ...

GROUP VIDEO DISCUSSION (15 MIN.)

1. Why does the message of Matthew 25 continue to be subversive to dominant social, political, and religious structures today?

2. What is Jesus' mission statement, according to his "Nazareth manifesto" declared in Luke 4:18 – 19?

3. Some people say that when the Bible refers to the "poor" we should interpret it as a reference to spiritual poverty. What is lost with this interpretation?

4. Some argue that the passage in Mark 14:7 in which Jesus says "For you always have the poor with you" means that Christians don't need to worry about the poor in this lifetime. What have you been taught about this passage? How does Jim Wallis interpret it? How does Wallis' interpretation fit in the context of the overall biblical message?

5. Why is it significant that Jesus was poor and homeless when he lived on this earth? How would Christianity be different if Jesus had been born into wealth and prosperity?

"Then the king will say to those at his right hand, 'Come, you that are blessed by my Father, inherit the kingdom prepared for you from the foundation of the world; for I was hungry and you gave me food, I was thirsty and you gave me something to drink, I was a stranger and you welcomed me, I was naked and you gave me clothing, I was sick and you took care of me, I was in prison and you visited me.' Then the righteous will answer him, 'Lord, when was it that we saw you hungry and gave you food, or thirsty and gave you something to drink? And when was it that we saw you a stranger and welcomed you, or naked and gave you clothing? And when was it that we saw you sick or in prison and visited you?' And the king will answer them, 'Truly I tell you, just as you did it to one of the least of these who are members of my family, you did it to me.'"

MATTHEW 25:34–40

GROUP BIBLE EXPLORATION AND APPLICATION (15 MIN.)

6. **Read:** Luke 4:18–19. A significant moment in Jesus' life and ministry, he specifically states that he has come to the earth to preach good news to the poor, release captives, and free the oppressed. If you read the gospel through the lens of this message, how might your view of Jesus' ministry change?

7. What are other moments in Jesus' ministry where he focused on the poor and the oppressed? Are there instances when he addresses wealth, prosperity, and power? Does he ever praise or commend these things?

8. **Read:** Matthew 25:31 – 46. According to this passage, how can Christians directly serve Jesus? Has service to the poor been emphasized as central to Christian conversion by the leaders in your church? What teaching have you received about the importance of ministry to and with the poor?

9. If you didn't know anything about the Bible and were trying to determine what is most important to Christianity in America right now, what would you say? Where would you get your information? After reading Jesus' "mission statement" in Luke 4:18 – 19 and reading Matthew 25, what do you think the Christian church's mission statement should be? How can that be made clear to all?

"Thank you, Lord, for waking me up this morning! That the walls of my room were not the walls of my grave and my bed was not my cooling board. Thank you, Lord! We know that you'll be coming through this line today, so Lord, help us to treat you well. Help us to treat you well."

MARY GLOVER

OPTIONAL GROUP ACTIVITY (8 – 15 MIN.)

Time permitting, break into groups of two or three and briefly discuss a time when you or someone you know was struggling with financial problems. Do not reveal how you or your friend were able to overcome this challenge or how people responded. Just give the context. What led up to it? What were the thoughts and emotions involved? Next, discuss how you might have responded to one another's situations, had you all known each other during that time. Then share how people actually responded to the real situation.

In the full group, address any of the following questions:

- For those who were shown great compassion, how did it feel to receive such a warm response in your time of trouble? For those who were not shown compassion, how did it feel to be neglected in your time of need?
- What are some principles of compassion that you can extrapolate from the stories that you shared together?
- Who are some people in your community (the homeless, struggling small-business owners, refugees, recent immigrants) who are as vulnerable as those in your stories? How might Jesus' mission statement be "good news" to them? How can your small group be living "good news" to them? Brainstorm three concrete ways in which your group can build relationships with vulnerable members of your community in big and small ways.
- Can your group commit to initiating, partnering with, or deepening these relationships during the weeks of this study? Remember that relationships are two-way streets. Dialogue means opening yourself up to listen to the heart and story of another, should they decide to share it with you.

> "This nation is affluent and has more than it needs. The realization that what we have is a free gift can deepen our desire to share this gift with others who cry out for help. When we bless the fruits of the harvest, let us at least realize that blessed fruits need to be shared."
>
> HENRI NOUWEN, *THE GENESEE DIARY*

CLOSING PRAYER (1 MINUTE)

The aim of this Bible study is to reveal more deeply God's heart for the poor. God knows our love for God through how we love the poorest, most vulnerable among us. Not only are we given the privilege as Christians of loving the poor, but we are also invited into deep relationships across economic lines. It is through these relationships that we discover the genuine good news of Jesus' message. Pray as a group that our affluence may always be set at the service of the needy and that our poverty always opens us to the good news of God.

TO DO ON YOUR OWN BETWEEN SESSIONS

- Read "Giving 'Burger King Mom' a Voice" by Jim Wallis (page 63 of the Appendix). Think of someone in your life who you know is struggling with financial issues or other needs. Spend time in prayer for this person, asking God to show you how best to be present to their needs. Reach out in a big or small way. Perhaps it's an email or a telephone call. Perhaps it's a week's worth of groceries. Whatever you do, do it with the love of God as your impetus and inspiration. If appropriate, brainstorm with the person about how they can take steps toward financial stability and ensure access to primary needs, such as food, shelter, and protection. Without revealing identities or breaking confidences, share your experience with your Bible study group next week.

- In preparation for the next session, read "The Gospel of Bling" by Robert M. Franklin (page 65 of the Appendix).

Is There Something Wrong with the "Prosperity Gospel"?

KEY ISSUE

Conspicuous wealth in the midst of great global poverty does not align with the heart of God.

The plight of the poor becomes particularly problematic in a time of prosperity. Despite an economic recession, we live in a wealthy nation with many resources available to us. For many Christians, it is difficult to avoid condemning the rich and expressing gracious, charitable compassion for the poor. As G. K. Chesterton said, "It may be possible to have a good debate over whether or not Jesus believed in fairies. It is a tantalizing question. Alas, it is impossible to have any sort of debate over whether or not Jesus believed that rich people were in big trouble — there is too much evidence on the subject and it is overwhelming."

It is ironic, then, that one of the largest and fastest-growing movements in modern-day Christianity is the "prosperity gospel" movement. Christians have grappled with their relationship to material goods and opportunities in this world since the first century. But in our era, something new and different has emerged. Today, prominent, influential, and attractive preachers and representatives of the church are advocates for financial prosperity. Perhaps this could only occur in a time and place where two conditions exist. First, Christianity is the dominant faith tradition, rather than an oppressed minority; second, the nation permits and rewards extraordinary inequalities of wealth and power.

The prosperity gospel may be even more insidious and dangerous because it subverts particular elements of Jesus' story and of biblical Christianity in order to instill a new attitude toward unfettered capitalism and conspicuous wealth. It often deliberately suppresses, ignores, or deletes language about radical sacrifice for the sake of God's kingdom. In other words, the prosperity gospel excludes a core message of the Jesus story, namely the cross. That symbol is an enemy to the confidence people place in material prosperity at the expense of trusting God. As the Bible clearly demonstrates, we must place our faith and confidence in the gospel of Jesus, not in material wealth.

Why are churches so susceptible to misreading or misplacing their moral compasses? The work that Jesus left for the church is clearly set forth in the New Testament, and the people he wants us to assist and empower are clearly identified. Moreover, Jesus provided the means for doing effective ministry before he departed. So what's the problem? In this session we will study the gospels, where Jesus strongly presses the rich in ways that should challenge us to reflect on wealth and its effects on the relationship between God and the poor. We will learn through an examination of various Bible passages that God provides prosperity as a means of sharing resources with entire communities, and that God doesn't mind prosperity, as long as it is put at the service of the most vulnerable. We also will tackle questions such as: What are the biblical and moral limits imposed on personal wealth and property? What are the obligations of Christians with regard to wealth, property, money, and assets in building a just economy?

WELCOME (1 MIN.)

God created each person on earth, knows each of us by name, and loves each of us. Human beings, on the other hand, often treat various groups of people as if they were less valuable than others, or less worthy of love. The God of the Bible takes a special interest in the poor, the marginalized, and the oppressed: The Lord hears the cry of the poor; blessed be the Lord (Psalm 34). Throughout the salvation story, God intervenes in human history to liberate the poor and oppressed and thus reveals the nature and will of God. We, too, as followers of

Jesus, must do the work of bringing justice to the poor, oppressed, and disenfranchised.

VIDEO TEACHING (20 MIN.)

Notes

The prosperity gospel is a heretical doctrine because ...

The early church mothers and fathers viewed wealth as a hindrance to faith because ...

The truth about a society is best known from the bottom because ...

In God's economy, there is enough for everyone, as long as ...

Christians must counter societal pressures that say, "Greed is good," "It's all about me," and "I want it now," with biblical statements such as ...

"Greed ... is not something wrong with gold; the fault is in a [person] who perversely loves gold and for its own sake abandons justice, which ought to be put beyond comparison above gold."

AUGUSTINE, *CITY OF GOD*

GROUP VIDEO DISCUSSION (15 MIN.)

1. According to early church fathers such as Ambrose, Clement of Alexandria, and Augustine, what must be done about our human desire for wealth? What did the early church teach about wealth?

2. According to some archaeological findings, what was the correlation between the gaps between rich and poor and the teachings of the prophets?

3. How can today's wealthy Christians faithfully manage their finances in a way that is pleasing to God?

> "A doctrine, a heresy, has seeped into the life of the church, called the prosperity gospel, that seems to say, 'If you have material wealth it could be a sign of God's favor and blessing, and by implication, if you don't, if you're poor, there might be something spiritually wrong with you.' ... [This] heresy ... needs to be confronted with the words of Jesus and the teachings of the early church."
>
> JIM WALLIS

4. What are some of the major problems with the "prosperity gospel," and how do the main tenets of this belief violate the true heart of God?

5. Talk about an experience you had that helped you to see the world from the perspective of those at the "bottom" of society. What were some of the injustices revealed to you through this experience?

6. How do we evaluate our society if we study it from the bottom? Is our society a just society? Why or why not?

"Then the LORD said, 'I have observed the misery of my people who are in Egypt; I have heard their cry on account of their taskmasters. Indeed, I know their sufferings, and I have come down to deliver them from the Egyptians, and to bring them up out of that land to a good and broad land, a land flowing with milk and honey, to the country of the Canaanites, the Hittites, the Amorites, the Perizzites, the Hivites, and the Jebusites. The cry of the Israelites has now come to me; I have also seen how the Egyptians oppress them."

EXODUS 3:7–9

GROUP BIBLE EXPLORATION AND APPLICATION (15 MIN.)

7. American culture pushes people to get more, to seek the illusion of full "control" of the future by attempting to control the present, and to attain security by amassing more money. **Read:** Luke 12:18. How does the image of "pull[ing] down barns and build[ing] larger ones" relate to the fostering of greed in American culture?

8. Biblical faith is an invitation away from anxiety and greed to the abundance of God. **Read:** Mark 6:34–44, the story of Jesus feeding the crowds with just five loaves and two fishes. How does this story challenge our present anxiety over providing security for ourselves through the acquisition of wealth?

9. **Read:** James 5:1 – 5. Why did James warn the rich to "weep and wail" because of impending misery? In a world with billions of people living in abject poverty, how should we define "wealthy"? How should wealthy people today heed James' warning?

10. Have you ever felt personally challenged by Jesus' teachings on wealth? How has economics affected relationships in your church — between members and in your neighborhood or town?

> "The lover of money will not be satisfied with money; nor the lover of wealth, with gain. This also is vanity. When goods increase, those who eat them increase; and what gain has their owner but to see them with his eyes?"
>
> ECCLESIASTES 5:10 – 11

OPTIONAL GROUP ACTIVITY (8 – 15 MIN.)

If you have time, choose *one* of these group experiences:

Activity #1

Cut one "extra" expenditure in your life for the rest of this Bible study. Examples might include your daily mocha latte, a Netflix subscription, eating out for lunch, or going to the movies. Pledge to fast from that expenditure and, together as a Bible study group, donate the money that would have been spent on that "extra" to a local ministry or charity. Find an organization that directly works with people who are poor in your community or neighborhood.

Activity #2

Divide your group into teams of two or three people. Assign each small group one of these things: a stack of magazines (any kind: current affairs, business, fashion, etc.), a television set to a news channel, or a computer set to show the current home page of a news website. For several minutes, look at the magazines, television content, or website and identify any references to personal "success." Then discuss any of the following:

- Based on your findings, what are the primary measures of personal success in our culture?
- Did you come across any references to helping the poor and oppressed?
- How do media portrayals of success impact you?
- Brainstorm ideas on how to avoid succumbing to the cultural norms around wealth and prosperity.

Activity #3

If you feel comfortable, break up into partner teams and, using paper and markers, create a basic circle diagram showing your monthly budget. For example, if you spend half of your budget on food, fill in half of the circle and write "food" in the section. Together discuss any of the following:

- What does your budget show about the priorities in your life?
- How does your partner's budget differ from yours? What can you learn from your partner's budgetary priorities?
- What would happen if you made a circle diagram out of the way you spend your time? Discuss with your partner what takes up most of the hours in your day and what that indicates about your priorities in life.
- How might you alter your financial budget or your time budget to more closely reflect the heart of God?

CLOSING PRAYER (1 MIN.)

The God of the Bible loves each person, regardless of economic status. In the Gospels, Jesus strongly presses the rich in a way that should challenge us today to reflect on wealth and its effect on relationships with God and with the poor. Pray that you will hold each other accountable as you press forward, seeking to imitate and follow God's heart for the poor and oppressed.

> "Remember that when you leave this earth, you can take with you nothing that you have received ... but only what you have given: a full heart, enriched by honest service, love, sacrifice, and courage."
>
> FRANCIS OF ASSISI

TO DO ON YOUR OWN BETWEEN SESSIONS

- Before every purchase that you make during this next week, ask yourself three questions: (1) does this purchase glorify God? (2) does this purchase aid my neighbor? (3) if this is a necessary expenditure, is there a way for me to acquire this item or service that better honors God and neighbor?

- In preparation for the next session, read "What the Heck Is 'Social Justice'?" by Rose Marie Berger (page 72 of the Appendix) and "The Overlooked Schism" by E. J. Dionne Jr. (page 75 of the Appendix).

Standing at the Corner
of Church and State

KEY ISSUE

**The church and the government both have
moral obligations to promote the good of society
within their respective limitations.**

Throughout Scripture we see that when people cannot care for themselves, the broader community has a responsibility to see that their needs are met. The people of God are called to care for the widow, the orphan, the stranger, and the "least of these." At different points in the biblical text, it is clear that the family has the first obligation to help needy members. When a family cannot support a needy relative, the church steps in. Any policy or political philosophy that immediately seeks governmental solutions for problems that could be solved just as well or better at the level of the family violates the biblical framework that stresses the central societal role of the family.

But what role should government play? Sin makes government intervention in the economy necessary. When selfish, powerful people deprive others of their rightful access to productive resources, the state rightly steps in with intervening power to correct the injustice. When other individuals and institutions in the community do not or cannot provide basic necessities for the needy, government rightly helps.

This teaching on the role of government applies not just to Israel in biblical times but to governments everywhere anytime. Government is an aspect of community and is inherent in human life as an expression of our created social nature. It is one leg of a three-legged stool that also includes the private sector and the church. The government must play its role in attending to the common good and ensuring that people aren't getting left out and left behind. Governmental action to empower the poor is one way we promote the common good and implement the truth that economic justice is a family affair. However, when indirect approaches are not effective in restraining economic injustice, providing economic opportunity to all, or providing care for those who cannot care for themselves, the state rightly acts to demand patterns of justice and provide vital services. And as Christians it is our responsibility to hold the government accountable. We can shape which direction government may go — whether it is a source of good for the people or whether it acts as an oppressive power. We must be a moral voice in the debates around public policy.

In this session we will discuss the democratic limits on governmental power and the attributes of good rulers characterized by justice and righteousness (that is, setting forth policies that advance justice for the weak and protect the poor). We will also discuss what our nation's budget, examined as a moral document, says about our country's values. Finally, we will learn from biblical examples that changing a country is not just about replacing one politician with another. The church must refrain from simply being a weathervane that points in whichever direction the wind is already blowing. Rather, it's important for us, as people of faith, to change the course of the wind when it blows in wrong ways by enacting social reform that will direct a nation and the world toward justice for the poor.

WELCOME (1 MIN.)

Thousands of years ago, the prophet Isaiah offered us God's vision of a good society. The vision includes fair wages, housing and health, safety and security. In America, people who work should not be poor, but today many are. We must ensure that all people who are able to work have jobs where they do not labor in vain. Economic security for our people is vital to our national security. Isaiah's vision links religious values with economic justice and moral behavior with political commitment. And it inspires the conviction that overcoming poverty must become a bipartisan commitment and a nonpartisan cause.

VIDEO TEACHING (20 MIN.)

Notes

God is personal, but never private because ...

The prophets rail against unjust rulers and governments because ...

The elements of the "three-legged stool" of civil society are ...

It is the church's role to demand justice from our government because ...

"God is personal, but never private."

JIM WALLIS

GROUP VIDEO DISCUSSION (15 MIN.)

1. Jim Wallis argues that God has a key role to play in the public spheres of government, the economy, and society at large. What

biblical examples does he cite to demonstrate that the God of the Bible cares about public things?

2. How can governments be disobedient to the will of God? What are some biblical examples of governments acting outside of God's will?

"Social advance depends as much upon the process through which it is secured as upon the result itself."
JANE ADDAMS (1860 – 1935), NOBEL PEACE PRIZE LAUREATE, SOCIAL WORKER, SOCIOLOGIST, AND SUFFRAGIST

3. Is it the role of the church to influence government policy? Explain your answer.

4. How can Christians best influence the government?

5. What are some historical examples of Christians pushing government toward enacting more godly policies?

"Never, never will we desist till we have wiped away this scandal from the Christian name, released ourselves from the load of guilt, under which we at present labor, and extinguished every trace of this bloody traffic, of which our posterity, looking back to the history of these enlightened times, will scarce believe that it has been suffered to exist so long a disgrace and dishonor to this country."

ANTI-SLAVERY CRUSADER WILLIAM WILBERFORCE

GROUP BIBLE EXPLORATION AND APPLICATION (15 MIN.)

6. **Read:** Romans 13:1–4. Who ultimately institutes legitimate rulers on this earth? Who do the righteous rulers serve? In this passage, what are some of the positive reasons for government, according to the apostle Paul? Does this passage allow for any open disagreement with those in power?

7. **Read:** Matthew 23. How does Jesus react to hypocrisy in religious authorities and church leaders? What does he tell people about practicing blind obedience or discerning obedience? What can we learn from Jesus' treatment of authority?

8. **Read:** Isaiah 58:6–14. What is the work that God desires from us? How are we to treat the homeless poor and those living in the

bonds of oppression? How are people of faith to work with government to bring justice to the poor?

"I am in Birmingham because injustice is here. Just as the prophets of the eighth century BC left their villages and carried their 'thus saith the Lord' far beyond the boundaries of their home towns... so am I compelled to carry the gospel of freedom beyond my own home town.... Moreover, I am cognizant of the interrelatedness of all communities and states. I cannot sit idly by in Atlanta and not be concerned about what happens in Birmingham. Injustice anywhere is a threat to justice everywhere."

MARTIN LUTHER KING JR., *LETTER FROM A BIRMINGHAM JAIL*

OPTIONAL GROUP ACTIVITY (8 – 15 MIN.)

Divide into several groups of two or three. In these small groups, select a current issue being discussed on Capitol Hill that requires a moral voice. Some examples include immigration reform, health care, poverty, creation care and environmental justice, and the value of life. In your groups, find passages in the Bible that might provide a moral perspective on these issues that goes beyond the politicking that often occurs on the Hill and in the media.

NOTE: As a body of believers, please practice sensitivity and openness with one another while discussing these controversial and often divisive topics. Avoid alienating people with differing perspectives by establishing some ground rules to allow for an open, but civil, exchange of ideas.

"Government support in the fight against poverty is crucial. Yet the year [of travel and observation] taught us never to sit back and rely on such commitments. Our politicians, in the final analysis, will follow our lead, not vice versa."

JEFFREY SACHS, *THE END OF POVERTY*

CLOSING PRAYER (1 MIN.)

The aim of this Bible study is to challenge you to think differently about your role and the government's role in addressing the scourge of poverty. Consider what lessons you've learned in the past three weeks. Pray together that God will continue to challenge you with new ideas and support you as you wrestle with these questions.

"The only way to live in any true security is to live so close to the bottom that when you fall you do not have far to drop, you do not have much to lose."

DOROTHY DAY, COFOUNDER OF THE
CATHOLIC WORKER MOVEMENT

TO DO ON YOUR OWN BETWEEN SESSIONS

- Write a letter to your member of Congress urging that he or she vote on upcoming legislation in a way that you think reflects the moral foundations outlined in the Bible. Commit to keeping up with legislation that requires a moral voice and join others from the church in calling our government to wise and just stewardship of the power that God has entrusted in them.

- In preparation for the next session, read "What the Waters Revealed" by Jim Wallis (page 83 of the Appendix).

The Gospel According to New Orleans

KEY ISSUE

The hidden secret of poverty in the United States was exposed by hurricanes Katrina and Rita.

Hurricane Katrina destroyed entire cities, the lives of more than a thousand people, the homes of hundreds of thousands, and the confidence of millions in the government's commitment and ability to protect them. Then Hurricane Rita reflooded New Orleans and caused millions to flee their refuges in Texas, including many who had already fled there from their homes in New Orleans. Much of New Orleans was emptied of its people, and broad areas of the Gulf Coast in Mississippi, Alabama, and Texas were devastated. More than one million people were displaced, and many around the nation took them in, some for a long time.

But the waters of Hurricane Katrina also washed away our national denial of the shockingly high number of Americans living in poverty and our reluctance to admit the still-persistent connection of race and poverty in America. It perhaps even eroded the political power of a conservative anti-social services ideology that, for decades now, has weakened the idea of the common good.

The pictures from New Orleans stunned the nation. They exposed the stark reality of who was suffering the most, who was left behind, who was waiting in vain for help to arrive, and who is now facing the most difficult challenges of recovery. The faces of those stranded in New Orleans were overwhelmingly poor and black, the very old and the very young. They were the ones who could not evacuate; had no cars or money for gas; no money for bus, train, or airfare; no budget for hotels or no friends or family with room to share or spare. They were already vulnerable before this calamity; afterward they were totally exposed and on their own. For days, nobody came for them. And the conditions of the places they were finally herded to ("like animals," many testified) sickened the nation. Those left behind in New Orleans had already been left out in America.

From the reporters covering the unprecedented disaster to ordinary Americans glued to their televisions, a shocked and even outraged response was repeated: "I didn't realize how many Americans were poor." Katrina revealed an invisible and often silent poverty that most of us in the richest nation on earth have chosen not to talk about, let alone take responsibility for. After the storm hit, we all saw it — and so did the rest of the world. It made Americans feel both compassion and shame. Many political leaders and commentators, across the ideological spectrum, acknowledged the national tragedy, not just of the horrendous storm but of the realities the flood waters exposed. And some have suggested that if the aftermath of Katrina finally leads the nation to demand solutions to the poverty of far too many of its citizens, then something good might come from this terrible disaster.

This session will examine what Americans learned about the state of the poor in the U.S. in the wake of hurricanes Katrina and Rita. What did the flood waters reveal about who is living in poverty? What systemic issues fuel poverty? Why has America gone backward in terms of lifting people out of poverty over the past thirty years?

WELCOME (1 MIN.)

Restoring the hope of America's poorest families, renewing our national infrastructures, protecting our environmental stability, and rethinking our most basic priorities will require nothing less than a national change of heart and direction. It calls for a transformation of political ethics and governance and a move from serving private interests to ensuring the public good. If Katrina changes our political conscience and reinvigorates among us a commitment to the common good, then even this terrible tragedy might be redeemed.

VIDEO TEACHING (20 MIN.)

Notes

The waters of Hurricane Katrina revealed ...

The faces of those stranded in New Orleans were overwhelmingly ...

As Christians, we should know what is happening ...

GROUP VIDEO DISCUSSION (15 MIN.)

1. What did you first feel when you saw the devastation of hurricanes Katrina and Rita? Do you know anyone who was living in the areas affected by the hurricanes? If so, share their stories with your group.

2. Did you participate in any of the mobilizations to send aid and volunteers to the Gulf Coast? If so, share with the group.

"Two babies have died, a woman died, a man died. We haven't had no food. We haven't had no water. We haven't had nothing."

UNIDENTIFIED KATRINA VICTIM, FROM
"KATRINA VICTIMS SHARE THEIR STORIES,"
NATIONAL PUBLIC RADIO

"The hardest part is, it didn't have to be this way. If people had evacuated—of course, where are they going to evacuate to? But other people did evacuate. Everybody that died here was needless. It's just the senselessness of it all."

DAVID CASH, A VOLUNTEER DOCTOR DURING HURRICANE
KATRINA, QUOTED IN THE NEW YORK TIMES

3. Jim Wallis says that the tragedy of Katrina can be redeemed if our nation would commit to breaking down the walls between the rich and the poor. What role did America's racial history play in who was most vulnerable when the hurricanes hit? What redemptive progress have you seen in the years following Katrina?

4. Where do you live in proximity to those struggling economically in your community? How might physical distance from those living in poverty affect one's heart for the poor?

5. Who are the most vulnerable members of our society right now? (Take into consideration our current economic and social climate.)

How might the church reach out to them? What can the church do to help break down the walls between the rich and the poor?

GROUP BIBLE EXPLORATION AND APPLICATION (15 MIN.)

6. **Read:** Nehemiah 2:11–18. In his speech to the people of Israel, Nehemiah says, "You see the trouble we are in, how Jerusalem lies in ruins with its gates burnt" (v. 17). What trouble do you see the city of New Orleans and the victims of Katrina in today?

7. What trouble is your own community in? What social struggles in your local community need "Nehemiahs" to rise up and point out the "trouble we are in"?

8. **Skim:** Nehemiah 3, where the text lists the various individuals and the tasks they accomplished in rebuilding Jerusalem. Jim Wallis says in the video that "everybody has an assignment at a place on the wall, a place in the city, and they, together, rebuild the wall that has fallen down." Rebuilding has to be a community-wide effort that maximizes each individual's gifts and talents. How might

your own group help rebuild New Orleans and the lives of Katrina victims while using everyone's gifts and talents?

9. How might your group help rebuild your community and work with those on the margins while using those gifts?

"Like the prophet Nehemiah, we stand ready to help 'rebuild the wall' (Nehemiah 2:17) that has crumbled in so many of our communities. But for that to work, the political will, moral resolve, and human and economic resources must be there to do the job. No one from the private or public sector can be allowed to opt out. In Washington, on a sunny spring day, we said, 'Let the building begin.'"

JIM WALLIS, ON "THE CRY FOR RENEWAL"
DELEGATION THAT MET ON MAY 23, 1995
TO PROMOTE CHRISTIAN SOCIAL CONCERN

OPTIONAL GROUP ACTIVITY (8 – 15 MIN.)

If you have enough time, choose *one* of these group experiences:

Activity #1

Spend some time praying for the victims of Hurricane Katrina. Remember the displaced, still living in trailers, waiting to return to their homes. Remember those who lost family to the hurricane. Remember those who lost their homes and have had to start their lives again. Remember the congregations that lost their churches.

Pray, also, for the hidden epidemic of poverty in the United States. Pray that the veil will be lifted and that believers and nonbelievers will work to end poverty, so that all people will have the resources to survive natural disasters.

Activity #2

Consider coming together at another time to watch the first hour of Spike Lee's excellent documentary *When the Levees Broke* (NOTE: There is some profanity in the testimonies and narrative of the documentary.) Discuss the film as a group:

- How did this documentary differ from the news coverage that you saw during Hurricane Katrina?
- Why is it important to hear the testimonies of the people who experienced Hurricane Katrina firsthand, who were evacuated from their homes and were staying in the Superdome? What is the importance of personal testimony?
- How did the government and the church respond correctly? What mistakes did the government and church make in response to Hurricane Katrina?

CLOSING PRAYER (1 MIN.)

The critical needs of poor and low-income families must become the first priority of federal and state legislatures, not the last. And, the blatant inequalities of race in America — especially in critical areas of education, jobs, health care, and housing — must now be addressed. Pray that God would free you from any legacy of prejudice or racism and give you a hunger and thirst for justice for all of God's beloved community.

> "Washing one's hands of the conflict between the powerful and the powerless means to side with the powerful, not to be neutral."
> PAULO FREIRE, CATHOLIC BRAZILIAN EDUCATOR

TO DO ON YOUR OWN BETWEEN SESSIONS

■ Examine your lifestyle and consider ways in which you can break down barriers between yourself and those less fortunate than you. Some examples might be to take public transportation instead of driving your car, shopping at a thrift store for the items you need rather than at big box stores, and serving at a shelter once a week. Acquaint yourself with the hardships that poor people in your community endure every day, and allow yourself to be inspired to help solve their problems with the resources you have access to.

■ In preparation for the next session, read "India on 20 Cents a Day" by Aseem Shrivastava (page 89 of the Appendix).

SESSION 5

"Outside the Gate": The Poor and the Global Economy

KEY ISSUE

**Christians have a responsibility to our brothers
and sisters all around the world.**

As Jim Wallis shared in his video teaching, in 2000 then-Chancellor Gordon Brown and Tony Blair of Great Britain became aware of the problem of global debt through an international coalition of activists known as Jubilee 2000, who called for the cancellation of Third World debt. Largely based in congregations and youth groups around the world, the Jubilee movement continued to grow with the increasing support of people in power such as Brown, Blair, and U2 lead singer Bono.

In June 2006, a group of American church leaders joined church leaders in the U.K. for a global poverty forum. Their main purpose: to lobby the G8 summit meeting on commitments needed to address the Millennium Development Goals — eight targets ranging from reducing extreme poverty and child mortality rates to fighting disease epidemics such as AIDS. Archbishop of Canterbury Rowan Williams hosted the meeting at Lambeth Palace. The U.S. delegation included Rich Cizik of the National Association of Evangelicals, George McKinney from the Church of God in Christ, Glenn Palmberg of the Evangelical Covenant Church, Ron Sider of Evangelicals for Social Action, Rich Stearns of World Vision, and Geoff Tunnicliffe of the World Evangelical Alliance, along with Sojourners' Jim Wallis, David Beckmann of Bread for the World, and representatives of mainline Protestant churches.

The group sent a letter urging President George W. Bush and leaders at the summit to "help the poorest people of the world fight poverty, AIDS, and hunger" and "cancel 100 percent of the debts owed by the poorest countries." The Jubilee campaign also lobbied for fair trade relations between wealthy and poor countries, and laws ensuring worker justice. Other evangelical signatories included Rick Warren, Brian McLaren, Max Lucado, Bill Hybels, Tony Campolo, and Leighton Ford. To those familiar with U.S. evangelicalism, the breadth of these names and the constituencies they represent shatters old assumptions.

Making the work of eliminating global poverty more difficult are conflicting, confusing ways of defining and talking about poverty. In our increasingly consumerist world, even global poverty figures must ultimately arrive in a wrapping that is not unattractive to the public. Trickle-down will ultimately work, we are repeatedly assured by growth economists. But faith in trickle-down, as John Kenneth Galbraith is said to have remarked, is a bit like feeding race horses superior oats so that starving sparrows can forage in their dung. All indications, especially in parts of the world such as rural India, are that a decade and a half of corporate globalization has left under-nutrition and malnutrition all but intact and might have worsened the predicament for many millions.

Even the ways that some officials *count* the poor can have a huge affect on efforts to address extreme poverty. For instance, by using a severely distorted measure like a poverty line pegged unreasonably low, public authorities and governments come up with grossly inaccurate reports on the number of people in poverty. If global poverty statistics are not disseminated accurately, the facts on the ground will only get worse — thanks to misinformed policy making, among other things. And the potential consequences across the globe could be nothing short of catastrophic.

While institutions such as the World Bank are commissioned with the goal of reducing poverty through low-interest or no-interest loans to developing countries, true justice for developing nations will only come when people of faith rise up to lobby governments and institutions for economic justice for the global poor. In this session we examine these consequences of misinformed policy making that ignores the reality that economics are relationships, and that our present-day global economics are killing poor people around the world. We will ask ourselves, how does a biblical reading of the global economy help us understand the roots of poverty worldwide? And how does the gospel instruct us to view our global economic relations with our brothers and sisters around the world?

WELCOME (1 MIN.)

As goes the U.S. economy, so goes the world economy. Christians serve in mission to the poor all around the world. For the first time in history, we have the information, knowledge, technology, and resources to bring the worst of global poverty virtually to an end. What we don't have is the moral and political will to do so, and it is becoming clear that it will take a new moral energy to create that political will.

VIDEO TEACHING (20 MIN.)

Notes

Global poverty is a concern ...

The U.S. economy is connected to ...

While the beneficiaries of globalization gain, the poor and oppressed ...

The poverty line for the global poor is ...

GROUP VIDEO DISCUSSION (15 MIN.)

1. Why is it a Christian imperative that we pay attention to the travails of the global poor? What are some ways in which the church has served the global poor?

2. How has globalization affected the poor around the world? How have U.S. policy decisions affected the process of globalization? What environmental effects has globalization had on the poor?

"Almost half the world — over 3 billion people — live on less than $2.50 a day.... In 2005, the wealthiest 20 percent of the world accounted for 76.6 percent of total private consumption [of the earth's resources]. The poorest 10 percent accounted for just 0.5 percent of total consumption, and the wealthiest 10 percent accounted for 59 percent of all the consumption."

WORLD BANK DEVELOPMENT INDICATORS, 2008

3. What are the Millennium Development Goals? What are some ways in which the church can help achieve these goals?

4. Jim Wallis tells the story of sharing about social justice with his two sons, Luke and Jack. How do you talk to the children and young people in your life about justice issues?

> "Every day, on average more than 26,000 children under the age of five die around the world, mostly from preventable causes. Nearly all of them live in the developing world or, more precisely, in 60 developing countries. More than one third of these children die during the first month of life, usually at home and without access to essential health services and basic commodities that might save their lives."
>
> "THE STATE OF THE WORLD'S CHILDREN," UNICEF, 2008

GROUP BIBLE EXPLORATION AND APPLICATION (15 MIN.)

5. **Read:** Leviticus 25:25–35. What does this text on the biblical concept of Jubilee say about a believer's responsibility to help the poor? What does the practice of Jubilee tell you about the character of God?

6. **Skim:** Deuteronomy 15. Consider the intent behind the years of Jubilee and years of debt release in Leviticus 25 and Deuteronomy 15. How might these passages speak to issues of global debt and those living in poverty? What are some practical personal steps we might take in the spirit of this biblical concept of Jubilee?

7. What, if anything, do these biblical teachings have to say to us today about international systems of indebtedness? Are we called to consider biblical principles as we approach questions such as international relations? Explain your answer.

"God is in the slums, in the cardboard boxes where the poor play house.... God is in the silence of a mother who has infected her child with a virus that will end both their lives.... God is in the cries heard under the rubble of war.... God is in the debris of wasted opportunity and lives, and God is with us if we are with them."

U2 LEAD SINGER BONO, AT THE NATIONAL PRAYER BREAKFAST, FEBRUARY 2, 2006

OPTIONAL GROUP ACTIVITY (8 – 15 MIN.)

If you have enough time, choose *one* of these group activities:

Activity #1

Gather random items from around the meeting room and see where they were made. Pick an item that was made in a country that is far from the United States. As a group, pray for the person or people who were involved in manufacturing this object. Though you may not know the details of how or in what conditions this item was made, you can pray for:

- The safety and well-being of the person/people who made the item.
- The righteousness and morality of the people who own the manufacturing companies. Pray that they would pay their workers fair wages and provide safe working conditions.
- The environment in which the object was made. Pray that environmental protection standards are enforced and that the local economy is not harmed by the creation, outsourcing, and exporting of the item to the United States.

Activity #2

Take a look at the current "Death and Taxes" poster that visually outlines the U.S. government budget (you can find it online at http://www.deathandtaxesposter.com). As a group, identify the three major expenses of the U.S. budget. For each, discuss:

- Does this expense promote the common good of domestic and global society?
- Does this expense protect the poor and oppressed members of society?
- Does this expense practice the morality outlined in the Bible?

CLOSING PRAYER (1 MIN.)

The global economy is a vast and complicated web of intersecting systems that often overlooks the poor and disenfranchised members of humanity. It is our responsibility, however, to uphold God's commandment to the people of all nations. We cannot stand blindly aside while globalization harms the environment, takes advantage of the poor, and continuously contributes to unjust economic inequality. We must take the time to research the global economy and work for the achievement of the Millennium Development Goals. Lift up prayers for how God wants you to be involved in this effort.

"My humanity is bound up in yours, for we can only be human together."
ARCHBISHOP DESMOND TUTU

TO DO ON YOUR OWN BETWEEN SESSIONS

- Do your best to find local products during your next trip to the grocery store. Or better yet, purchase all of your groceries at a farmers market for the next week or two. Support your local economy in lieu of supporting large corporations that import their goods and labor from poorer countries that might not have stringent labor and environmental protection laws. Supplement your "local" shopping with activism for fair trade and protection of the world's poor. Find and support an organization or a petition that advocates for a more just global economy.

- In preparation for the next session, read "The Roots of Justice Revival" by Jim Rice (page 91 of the Appendix).

From Serial Charity to a Just Society

KEY ISSUE

The deeper theological issue is not *whether* but *how* Christians should engage with those who are poor in bringing about greater human dignity and justice.

Every single social movement in our country has had people of faith at the core. The abolition of slavery, women's suffrage, and civil rights are movements that all started when Christians heeded God's call to bring justice to the poor. Throughout religious history, numerous movements have brought justice and morality back to the center of society. People such as Charles Finney, John Wesley, Phoebe Palmer, Emeline Dryer, and Martin Luther King Jr. were deeply involved in reform efforts regarding temperance, the role of women, peacemaking, racial justice, and many other issues of the day. Today's movements for human rights and social justice are very much rooted in the faith traditions represented in the list of people above, a fact that is too little acknowledged by many who are successors to this legacy.

The false dichotomy of recent decades — that one kind of Christian talks about "evangelism" and "revival" and another kind altogether focuses on justice — is beginning to crack. Many Christians today have rediscovered the heritage of the nineteenth-century revivalist reformers. Many Christians — from all strands of the church, mainline and evangelical, Protestant and Catholic — have come to understand that working for social justice is a constitutive aspect of the gospel and that "withdrawal" from the world is not an option. They have come to see, as Charles Finney put it, "The Christian church has it in her power to reform this nation.... No [nation] has had strength to resist any reform which God's people have unitedly demanded."

In this final session, we will consider what implications God's call to do the right thing by the poor has for our personal, church, and societal economic and civic priorities. Jesus didn't treat those who were destitute, marginalized, or sick in a patronizing manner. Instead, he invited them to a new life, which included participating in their own liberation. Likewise, people of faith today must initiate social movements that make change possible. We must work to change the wind, using the different gifts represented in our faith communities to meet the crushing needs of the world.

How will you answer God's call to work for justice in the world today? How will you move from a place of personal revival to bringing global revival that breaks down oppression and uplifts the poor and marginalized?

WELCOME (1 MIN.)

Some think we can change poverty just by helping poor people in our families, churches, and neighborhoods, or by doing economic development in the community. These services do provide vital aid for many people — it is important to shelter the homeless, feed the hungry, and engage in development projects abroad. Others think all we must do to address poverty is to lobby and talk to members of Congress. But neither charity nor advocacy alone is adequate. What will truly change things is nothing less than a movement, a social movement. And faith has been at the center of every single social reform movement in our nation's history.

VIDEO TEACHING (20 MIN.)

Martin Luther King Jr. pushed President Johnson to enact the civil rights laws by ...

Social movements make change possible through ...

Spiritual activity doesn't get to be called "revival" until it changes ...

Renewal is ...

Revival is ...

GROUP VIDEO DISCUSSION (15 MIN.)

1. In the video Jim Wallis discusses the differences between renewal and revival. Talk about the differences between the two within your group. What have you seen evidence of in your own faith community — renewal or revival?

2. Martin Luther King Jr. used the power of the faith community to push President Lyndon Johnson to enact a civil rights law for the black community. How is the civil rights movement an example of the faith community bringing revival to the land?

"Any religion that professes to be concerned about the souls of [people] and is not concerned about the slums that damn them, the economic conditions that strangle them, and the social conditions that cripple them is a spiritually moribund religion."

MARTIN LUTHER KING JR.

3. What problem was affecting the Columbus, Ohio, churches before the Justice Revivals began? What was the "disconnect" that Jim Wallis pointed out in his discussion with church leaders?

4. Do you see a similar disconnect in the neighborhoods surrounding your faith communities? Explain.

5. Within your Bible study group, discuss how you might be able to bring full revival into your community, much like the Ten Point Coalition did through their efforts to stop youth homicide in Bos-

ton. Strategize ways in which you can partner with local churches and local government to bring revival to your city.

"The kingdom of God is justice and peace
and joy in the Holy Spirit.
Come, Lord, and open in us
the gates of your kingdom."
HYMN FROM TAIZÉ, AN ECUMENICAL
MONASTIC COMMUNITY IN FRANCE

GROUP BIBLE EXPLORATION AND APPLICATION (15 MIN.)

6. **Read:** Mark 1:40–45. In Jewish law, touching a diseased person was grounds for becoming "unclean." Why is it significant that Jesus touched the leper to heal him? In this first healing of Jesus' ministry, how does Jesus confront the social traditions of his time that allowed for people like the leper to remain on the fringes of society?

7. How might Christians today also buck the status quo and touch the poor and oppressed members of society to bring them justice? What are some of the systemic causes of poverty that the church can help dismantle?

8. **Read:** Luke 4:16–30. As mentioned in an earlier session, this passage is where Jesus announces his mission to the world. If you were to announce your mission to the world (or, at least, to this Bible study group), what would you say?

9. How can you turn the personal renewal you've experienced in this Bible study to corporate revival? How can your Bible study group turn renewal into community-wide revival?

OPTIONAL GROUP ACTIVITY (8 – 15 MIN.)

If you have enough time, choose *one* of these group experiences:

Activity #1

Share with one another about the effects this study has had on your theology, decisions, and lifestyle.

- What has been the most difficult group activity or "To Do on Your Own" experiment?
- What do you disagree about with Christians and poverty in this study?
- What do you still have questions about?
- What has been a positive change to occur in your life during this study?
- What, if any, further application is there for you or your church that you'd like to share and discuss with your group?

Activity #2

Join together to form a social justice-focused local coalition or do research to find an organization in your community that your group's members can agree to get involved in. Here are some ideas:

- Find ways to respectfully meet people who are poor in your community and learn about their struggles. Make contacts with local community service groups and shelters to ask about volunteer opportunities.
- Identify the systemic causes of poverty in your own community and brainstorm ways you might address some of these root causes.
- Pledge to meet once a week to pray for renewal and justice to come to your community.
- Make dates to shop at local farmers markets together. Talk to the farmers to find out the needs of the local farming community.
- Develop a relationship with your local government and municipalities. Attend town hall meetings together. Become actively engaged in the local government, and push for actions that will help the poor and disadvantaged members of your community.

"Every spiritual master in every tradition talks about the significance of small things in a complex world. Small actions in social life, small efforts in the spiritual life, small moments in the personal life. All of them become great in the long run, the mystics say, but all of them look like little or nothing in themselves."

JOAN CHITTISTER, ORDER OF SAINT BENEDICT

CLOSING PRAYER (1 MIN.)

The one we claim as Lord and Savior was materially poor and yet he was able to change the world. We do not need money or power to change the world. Instead, we must enter the world as Jesus did, taking up the burden of the poor, inviting them to a new life of justice and freedom and to participation in their own liberation.

As you conclude, read aloud together the Prayer of Saint Francis. Pray these words to one another as a pledge to uphold God's heart for those living in poverty and in the margins of society. Offer this prayer to God in thanksgiving for the gift of this time of study and for the passion to put faith into action.

Lord, make me an instrument of your peace; where there is hatred, let me sow love; where there is injury, pardon; where there is doubt, faith; where there is despair, hope; where there is darkness, light; and where there is sadness, joy.

O God, grant that I may not so much seek to be consoled as to console; to be understood, as to understand; to be loved, as to love; for it is in giving that we receive, it is in pardoning that we are pardoned, and it is in dying that we are born to Eternal Life. Amen.

TO DO ON YOUR OWN IN THE COMING DAYS

- Write out a pledge on paper, applying the lessons you learned during this study, about how to serve those who are living in poverty and to honor God's call to be with the poor. Pledge to serve the poor in the ways that impressed you most during this study. Sign and date your pledge and display it in a public place in your home or office.

"St. Benedict tells me to run to Christ. If I stop for a moment and consider what is being asked of me here, and what is involved in the act of running, I think of how when I run I place first one foot and then the other on the ground, that I let go of my balance for a second and then immediately recover it again. It is risky, this matter of running. By daring to lose my balance I keep it."
ESTHER DE WAAL, *LIVING WITH CONTRADICTION: AN INTRODUCTION TO BENEDICTINE SPIRITUALITY*

APPENDIX

Giving "Burger King Mom" a Voice, by Jim Wallis

The Gospel of Bling, by Robert M. Franklin

What the Heck Is "Social Justice"? by Rose Marie Berger

The Overlooked Schism, by E. J. Dionne Jr.

What the Waters Revealed, by Jim Wallis

India on 20 Cents a Day, by Aseem Shrivastava

The Roots of Justice Revival, by Jim Rice

Giving "Burger King Mom" a Voice

BY JIM WALLIS

She was working the drive-through window at four in the afternoon. But whenever there was a lull between orders, the young woman returned to a table in the corner of the local Burger King. Three kids were sitting there, with schoolbooks, papers, and pencils all spread out, doing their homework. And mom was helping as best she could while keeping straight the orders for Whoppers, fries, and chicken nuggets.

Given her low wages, this single mother was no doubt balancing more than fast food and homework; she was also deciding between paying the rent, going to the doctor and getting prescriptions when somebody gets sick — or worrying about winter boots for her kids. I call her "Burger King Mom."

"Soccer moms" and "NASCAR dads" have received much attention in recent election campaigns. But who will speak to or for Burger King Mom? She may live in a red or blue state, but neither party is much interested in her or her family's issues. She is part of the low-income demographic most unrepresented in U.S. politics, with the lowest levels of both voter registration and turnout — and with a high percentage of immigrants. Many low-income people have a hard time connecting to voting: It's too complicated; there are too many other things to worry about; and there is too little reason for confidence that the outcome will make much difference for them. The Republicans look after their wealthy constituents, and the Democrats want to be the champions of the middle class. Neither makes a priority of the needs of the poor. Is that because the problems of poverty are disappearing in America? Hardly. The poverty rate (including that for children) rose in 2002 and 2003. More people than ever are without health insurance. Increasing numbers of people can't find affordable housing. The minimum wage hasn't been raised since 1997.

George Bush's faith-based initiative has been reduced to a photo op, while domestic spending that most affects the poor has been drastically cut in favor of war, homeland security, and tax cuts that mostly benefit the rich. The media have yet to report on the condition of low-income American families, who have also become the casualties of war. We need to redefine the poverty issue as one of growing income inequality in America, and one that increasingly affects working families. American inequality is in 2004 greater than at any time since the roaring injustice of the 1920s or the rampant wealth and poverty of the Gilded Age in the nineteenth century. The Bush administration's tax policies seem deliberately aimed at returning to the wealth distribution of those periods. But, especially since the 1990s, both parties are following the dictates of their corporate donors more than the dictates of compassion or justice. The Republicans run as compassionate conservatives and then govern as corporatists, while the Democrats run as populists, then also govern as corporatists.

Most Americans believe that if you work hard and full time, you should not be poor. But the truth is that many working families are, and many low-income breadwinners must hold down multiple jobs just to survive. With stagnant wages in an economy that is growing for some but clearly not for others, more and more people and their children are simply being left out and left behind. What is at risk is the reality of a genuine opportunity society and the ethic of work when work no longer is enough to support a family.

The good news is that religious leaders and communities from across the theological and political spectrum are responding to the vacuum of political leadership on poverty and income inequality. In fact, poverty is becoming the defining moral issue for many in the faith community — including evangelicals and Pentecostals as well as Catholics, mainline Protestants, and the black churches. While divided on other issues such as gay marriage and abortion, some church leaders are displaying a determined "unity" to make poverty a religious issue in elections. Maybe Burger King Mom will have somebody speaking for her and her kids after all.

Jim Wallis is editor-in-chief of Sojourners. *This article appeared in the June 4, 2005 issue of* SojoMail.

The Gospel of Bling

BY ROBERT M. FRANKLIN

I am convinced that the single greatest threat to the historical legacy and core values of the contemporary black church tradition is posed by what is known as the "prosperity gospel" movement. That movement, however, is only symptomatic of a larger mission crisis or "mission drift" that has placed the black church in the posture of assimilating into a culture that is hostile to people living on the margins of society, such as people living in poverty, people living with AIDS, homosexuals, and immigrants.

This is not a new challenge. Christians have grappled with their relationship to material goods and opportunities in this world since the first century. But in our era something new and different has emerged. Today, prominent, influential, and attractive preachers and representatives of the church now are advocates for prosperity. Perhaps this could only occur at a time and in a place where two conditions exist. First, Christianity is the dominant faith tradition; second, the nation permits and rewards extraordinary inequalities of wealth and power.

The gospel of assimilation provides sacred sanction for personal greed, obsessive materialism, and unchecked narcissism. That distorted gospel dares not risk a critique of the culture and systems that thrive in the presence of a morally anemic church. This is more than a concern about the encroachment of the prosperity gospel movement that receives so much negative attention. Rather, this is a more thorough and comprehensive distortion of the religion of Jesus.

To be a successful (different from faithful) pastor in today's world is to confront the ever-present temptation to sell one's soul, compromising one's vocation and ethical responsibilities, in exchange for or access to wealth. One Houston-based minister observed that when the church gets a mortgage, "poor people" become just another church program. Poor people were central to Jesus' own self-definition, but they are often relegated to one of many service programs of today's corporate church, simply another item on the services menu.

The tragedy is that one-fourth of the black community lives in poverty while many clergy and churches are distracted and seduced by the lure of material wealth. When churches devote more time to building their local kingdoms and less time to nurturing and uplifting poor people, they are struggling with a mission crisis.

A PROSPERITY FIELD TRIP

One Sunday, I visited the church of my Atlanta neighbor, the Rev. Creflo Dollar. I had heard about the burgeoning ministry of the World Changers Church and felt I should see for myself.

I found a parking space three blocks from the sanctuary. The hike to the sanctuary was so far that I momentarily forgot where I was headed and began to window shop the stores en route to the church, perhaps unconsciously getting into prosperity mode. I finally arrived and entered the enormous domed sanctuary, taking a seat near the front. Everything was neat and comfortable. The blue carpet and plush pew covers were welcoming. The huge rotating globe and other props on stage subtly reminded one that what happens here is intended for a global television audience.

After the choir sang, Rev. Dollar entered the sanctuary dressed in a business power suit and took his seat. Most black preachers begin their sermons in a conversational way. They acknowledge the presence of special guests and familiar faces and invite people to relax and laugh before they begin the journey toward an encounter with the holy. But this was a bit different, perhaps because the stage lights and television cameras were operating. Dispensing with all of the "old school" black church conventions, he went right to the text for the day.

The first 15 minutes of his message were encouraging and impressive. I heard evidence of a critical thinker who had done his homework and given careful attention to various scholarly sources for the selected biblical text. Then, out of nowhere, he began to testify about a friend who had recently given him a second Rolls Royce. He continued, "Now, that's not the Rolls that you all gave me years ago. See, so don't get mad. This was a gift from a friend." I wonder if anyone else wondered, "Why does he need one Rolls Royce? But, two?"

More amazing was that the congregation seemed to affirm this testimony of personal indulgence and excess. No one seemed to have the power to hold the preacher accountable for exceeding his proper allowance as a representative of Jesus. I do not know Rev. Dollar personally and I will reserve judgment about his motives and character, but it appears he has followed the script for how a successful and affluent corporate executive behaves. He does not seem to have entertained the possibility of rewriting that script and offering to other ministers and followers a new paradigm of socially responsible affluence.

If most black preachers — and other preachers for that matter — are preoccupied with pursuing the "bling-bling" life of conspicuous consumption, then poor people are in big trouble, because it indicates that the hearts of their chief advocates are "drunk with the wine of the world," to use James Weldon Johnson's phrase, and incapable of speaking truth to power.

Given the distorting influence of the prosperity movement on authentic Christianity, I should say more about the phenomenon.

We should distinguish between three realities: First, the "gospel of prosperity." Second, the "prosperity gospel." And third, radical Christian stewardship that may include the ownership of material goods.

The gospel of prosperity: "Greed is good." The "gospel of prosperity" refers to the cultural ideology that suggests that the accumulation of material possessions, wealth, and prosperity are morally neutral goods that are necessary for human happiness. I characterize it as an ideology rather than merely an idea because it functions like a powerful, unconscious force that does not revise its position in the face of counterevidence. For instance, its advocates would not admit that possessing material goods in excess may actually induce unhappiness. As an ideology, its believers insist upon its correctness, deny the legitimacy of other perspectives, and pursue wealth without concern for long-term consequences. Prosperity becomes an intrinsic good and an end in itself.

Most examples of this vulgar form of material worship do not pretend to be religious, certainly not Christian. Rather, they are elements of what might be called America's largest quasi-religious tradition, namely the religion of capitalism. The gospel of prosperity has been a guiding ideology or myth embodied in the Horatio Alger story (among others), where people acquire wealth through the heroic exercise of risk-taking, ingenuity, high energy, inordinate self-confidence, and tireless effort. That's the gospel of prosperity that underwrites American capitalism. The gospel of prosperity is a competitor to authentic Christianity (and other faith traditions) and ruthlessly seeks to establish its preeminence in the culture.

THE PROSPERITY GOSPEL OF THE SPIRITUAL ENTREPRENEURS

The "prosperity gospel" asserts that Christian faith is an investment that yields material abundance. Rev. Dollar fits in this category, along with scores of other televangelists who live and instruct others on how to "think and grow rich." Wealth is outward proof of an inner grace and righteousness. Salvation is both spiritual and material. And although the "prosperity gospel" may not be as vulgar an expression of greed as the "gospel of prosperity," both are corrosive and threatening to American churches, which are constantly tempted to focus on their own institutional well-being at the expense of serving the vulnerable.

The prosperity gospel may be even more insidious and dangerous because it subverts particular elements of the Jesus story and of classical biblical Christianity in order to instill a new attitude toward capitalism and riches. It often deliberately suppresses, ignores, and/or deletes language about radical sacrifice for the sake of God's kingdom. In other words, it excludes a core message of the Jesus story, namely that which is symbolized by the cross. That symbol is an enemy to the underlying confidence people invest in material prosperity at the expense of trusting God. "Cross talk" insists that believers share their material prosperity rather than hoard it. At times the call to share wealth may be so radical that a person is compelled to give it all away in order to serve and please God.

I refer to the clergy who operate from this orientation as "spiritual entrepreneurs" who know how to produce, package, market, and distribute user-friendly spirituality for the masses. The spiritual product lines they market rarely make stringent ethical demands upon their listeners. Instead, they proffer a gospel of health, wealth, and success designed to help others become more affluent. When these leaders serve as pastors of congregations, they function like "entrepreneurial ecclesiastical executives" at the helm of corporate organizations. Such congregations and leaders may be changing who they are and are called to be, distorting the meaning of church as a community of holy awareness, care, interdependence, sharing, moral deliberation, and action.

PROPHETIC STEWARDSHIP

A third view of faith and money is "prophetic stewardship." I use the word prophetic to emphasize that this model represents something of a negative judgment on its alternatives, the secular gospel of prosperity and the pseudo-religious prosperity gospel. It seeks to displace them with a more radical version of stewardship and shared prosperity. Here it is understood that the Christian gospel includes many goods — spiritual, social, psychological, physical, and material. But none of them, apart from the spiritual good of salvation, is promised without qualification. Again, the cross and a disciple's faithful embrace of it may require one to practice what theologian Jacquelyn Grant has called an "ethic of renunciation," in which we may have to sacrifice physical well-being, psychological comfort, social support, and material goods for the sake of saving our souls. Is this the meaning of Matthew 6:33 (KJV), "But seek ye first the kingdom of God, and his righteousness; and all these things shall be added unto you"?

Prophetic stewardship invites reflection upon the meaning of the values found in passages such as Matthew 6:19 – 20. There, Jesus engages in "cross talk" as he declares "do not store up for yourselves treasures on earth where moth and rust destroy and where thieves break in and steal, but store up for yourselves treasures in heaven." Acts 2:44 – 45 indicates that "All the believers were together and had everything in common. Selling their possessions and goods, they gave to anyone as he had need" (NIV). When people had a life-changing encounter with Jesus, it also reshaped their attitude toward their possessions.

Prophetic stewardship is the most adequate and authentic expression of a Christian orientation to money. Consequently, Christians should aspire to understand, accept, and practice prophetic stewardship. Such stewardship both encourages Christians to live in a simple but comfortable manner (leaving a small footprint on the earth) and publicly works to change the culture's prevailing habits of greed. This public move is what makes it prophetic. That is, prosperity per se should never become a prominent theme or mark of the faithful Christian life. It should never compete with the cross for center stage. Material acquisition should always be incidental to one's vocation and one must always be prepared to make radical sacrifices for the sake of one's soul and/or the good of the reign of God.

Against the background of the prosperity gospel movement and the seductions of spiritual leaders is the more chilling report that many churches located in high poverty neighborhoods are not responding to local needs effectively. R. Drew Smith, a senior fellow at the Leadership Center of Morehouse College, undertook research in four cities on the relationship between churches and low-income residents. His 2003 report, "Beyond the Boundaries: Low-Income Residents, Faith-Based Organizations and Neighborhood Coalition Building," states the following conclusions:

Two-thirds of the housing complex residents surveyed report having little or no contact with faith-based organizations in the previous year; many congregations report having programs of potential value to neighborhood residents but indicate that church members take advantage of these programs more frequently than nonmembers; and, roughly two-thirds of the congregations report that most of their members live more than one mile from their place of worship.

Smith and others underscore the social isolation of low-income, urban residents from the jobs, social services, and poverty-alleviating networks in their metro areas. And he points to the potential of churches to bridge that distance and help to connect people and their communities.

I hope that the disconnect between churches and their local neighborhoods will become an issue that evokes conversation about how congregations that do little for local residents can revise their ministries to serve them more effectively. And I hope that the same community that criticizes inactive churches will acknowledge and reward those that are active and faithful to their mission.

Why are churches so susceptible to misreading or misplacing their moral compasses? The work that Jesus left for the church is clearly set forth in the New Testament, and the people he wanted us to assist and empower are clearly identified. Moreover, Jesus provided the means for doing effective ministry before he departed. So what's the problem? I would submit that leadership, its quality, performance, and education, are essential.

The irony is that many black preachers stylistically present themselves to the world as large, powerful, and accomplished individuals. How many of today's denominational leaders, local pastors, or founders of the new megachurches have risked their access to important people or revenue streams in order to achieve goals in the arena of social justice, such as dismantling penalties against the working poor, expanding health-care coverage, or dramatically improving the well-being of children?

We must invite and challenge leaders to do the right things, to do them more effectively, and in a collaborative manner. Further, we should reward institutions and leaders that meet our expectations and ignore those who are unresponsive or deliberately clueless. Moreover, we should actively isolate, stigmatize, and discourage those who are harmful to our communities. This must never be done in a mean-spirited way, but we must not permit leaders who exploit people to think that the community approves of such poor stewardship. The community deserves prophetic stewards.

Robert M. Franklin was the presidential distinguished professor of social ethics at the Candler School of Theology at Emory University and president of the Regional Council of Churches of Atlanta when this article appeared in the January 2007 issue of Sojourners *magazine. This article is adapted from* Crisis in the Village: Restoring Hope in African-American Communities *(Fortress Press).*

What the Heck Is "Social Justice"?

BY ROSE MARIE BERGER

Every seventh year, according to biblical tradition, the people of God are invited to observe a "Year of Remission" (*Shmita*, in Hebrew). It is a year in which land and crops and domesticated animals rest, when creditors refrain from collecting debts, and when the Law of the Lord is read in the hearing of all (marking the completion of the Torah liturgical cycle).

These ancient biblical customs and covenants form the foundation for the Christian concept of social justice. In Christian tradition, particularly Catholic teaching, social justice and social charity form the horizontal axis, and individual justice and individual charity form the vertical axis. All four elements work in harmony for individuals and communities to live out the commandment: Love God and love your neighbor as yourself.

Justice is the moral code that guides a fair and equitable society. When an individual acts on behalf of justice, he or she stands up for what is right. Charity is a basic sense of generosity and goodwill toward others, especially the suffering. Individual charity is when one responds to the more immediate needs of others — volunteering in a women's shelter, for example.

The goal of social charity and social justice is furthering the common good. Social charity addresses the effects of social sin, while social justice addresses the causes of such sins. Brazilian Catholic Archbishop Hélder Câmara famously said, "When I feed the poor, they call me a saint; when I ask why they are poor, they call me a communist." His phrase indicates the societal pressure to separate charity and justice. The two cannot be separated. It would be like taking the heart out of a body — neither would live for long.

Social charity is sometimes called compassionate solidarity. A church's decision to buy only fair trade coffee might be considered an act of social charity. It is a communal economic act that addresses the immediate needs of those who are oppressed by an unjust economic system. However, it doesn't fundamentally change or challenge the unjust structure.

The principle of social justice, according to Catholic social teaching, requires the individual Christian to act in an organized manner with others to hold social institutions accountable — whether government or private — to the common good. The "common good comprises the sum total of social conditions which allow people, either as groups or as individuals, to reach their fulfillment more fully and more easily," according to Pope Paul VI. However, social justice can become hollow if it is not constantly in touch with real people's experiences.

Social justice issues are determined by "discerning the signs of the times" (Matthew 16:3), a careful process of social analysis. First, we listen to and observe the experiences of those closest to the problem. Second, together with those closest to the problem, we look at the context. What's the history and what are the root causes? Are there political and/or cultural forces at play? We take the expanded information (experience plus context) and examine it in light of biblical values and Christian teaching. What would Jesus do in a situation like this? Third, we ask: What action might successfully make this situation more just? Finally, we take the action and evaluate the results. The evaluation takes us back to step one.

Social justice almost always has an economic, as well as a policy, component. Our lives are organized around basic goods and services that we exchange in order to grow as healthy human beings in families and communities. When we listen to the experiences of poor people in the U.S., for example, we learn that many are working full-time but can't afford the basics of food, housing, and health care. The context includes spiraling costs of medical insurance and an inadequate federal minimum wage. We reflect on the experience and context in the light of Jesus' healing ministry and Jesus' parable of the worker getting a just wage. Campaigns for health care reform and a living wage have arisen from such analysis. Success is evaluated by how the lives of America's working poor have improved. Have these actions helped to restore justice and reveal more clearly the reign of God?

The Sabbath Year is a good time to review (and renew) the social justice ethic of the church. Salvation Army leader Evangeline Booth's comments on the women's movement in 1930 are pertinent for social justice movements today. For what we call the movement, she says, "is not social merely, not political merely, not economic merely. It is the direct fulfillment of the gospel of the Redeemer."

Rose Marie Berger was an associate editor of Sojourners *magazine when this article appeared.*

The Overlooked Schism

BY E. J. DIONNE JR.

The core divisions among religious Americans, and particularly Christians, are no longer defined by theological issues. The splits are political. The friendly (or at least usually friendly) arguments among believers over back fences and at kitchen tables or backyard barbeques tend not to focus on the Virgin Birth, the real presence of Jesus in the Eucharist, infant baptism, or the nature of the Trinity. More often, they are about issues such as abortion and gay marriage — and about attitudes toward government.

This has led to a peculiar kind of ecumenism. Historically, the defining religious divisions in our politics have been between Protestants and Catholics and between Christians and Jews. (Muslims have arrived to our shores in significant numbers only relatively recently.) In largely homogenous Protestant communities, there were also fierce feuds among denominations, particularly between Methodists and Baptists in smaller Southern towns. As in so many things in our history, racial divisions affected all groups. And many Protestant denominations split along regional lines around the issues of the Civil War. But on the whole, social and theological differences between denominations and faith traditions mattered a great deal.

Those old divisions have largely passed away. Now, conservative Catholics, Protestants, and Jews tend to ally together against liberal Catholics, Protestants, and Jews. As Grant Wacker, a professor of church history at Duke Divinity School, has said: "One of the most remarkable changes of the twentieth century is the virtual evaporation of hostility between Protestants and Catholics. I don't think it's because Baptists have come to have a great respect for Tridentine theology. It's because they see Catholics as allies against graver problems. There's a large reconfiguration going on now." Wacker was speaking mostly of the conservative side of politics, but his words apply to moderates and liberals as well.

It's common to talk about these divisions in relation to gay rights and abortion, and those differences are real. The gay rights issue in particular has led to great contention within many of our Protestant denominations. Less prominent in media accounts, but at least as important, is the sharp difference among believers over government's role in dealing with major social challenges, including the four themes of this special issue: poverty, the environment, public health, and disaster relief. The split over government is the Overlooked Schism.

The argument is not, for the most part, about the individual obligation to charity toward the least among us nor, in principle at least, about the biblical call to justice. The Old and New Testaments are abundantly clear in demonstrating what the Catholic Church has called "a preferential option for the poor." Isaiah speaks of undoing the heavy burdens and letting the oppressed go free. And as Jim Wallis has long argued, to ignore Jesus' preaching about the poor is to eviscerate the gospel message.

But there is a powerful dispute over what modern government, as against individuals, should do to lift up the poor. There is contention over the relative importance of social and individual responsibility. If religious progressives tend to criticize government for being insufficiently generous toward the poor, religious conservatives argue that too much government assistance promotes dependency.

Take, for example, President George W. Bush's strong words about the poor in his first inaugural address. He said: "In the quiet of the American conscience, we know that deep persistent poverty is unworthy of our nation's promise. And whatever our views of its cause, we can agree that children at risk are not at fault." So far he has everybody around the table with him, seated from left to right.

Then Bush said this: "Abandonment and abuse are not acts of God, they are failures of love. And the proliferation of prisons, however necessary, is no substitute for hope and order in our souls."

Now given his record on law and order issues, it's moving for Bush even to bring up the proliferation of prisons as a problem. But what's important is where he locates the cause of these social difficulties: abandonment and abuse are the problems for these poor children; hope and order in our souls is the solution to the problem of criminality.

Bush also declared: "Compassion is the work of a nation, not just a government. And some needs and hurts are so deep they will only respond to a mentor's touch or a pastor's prayer. Church and charity, synagogue and mosque lend our communities their humanity, and they will have an honored place in our plans and in our laws."

Again, there is much that religious people of various philosophical persuasions would applaud, but, whatever it is, it is not exactly the old social gospel or the New Deal.

For many progressives, the emphasis lies elsewhere. "It takes a village," the title of Hillary Rodham Clinton's book, comes from Africa, but it well could arise out of the social justice tradition in Methodism, and the religious progressive tradition generally. Clinton's view of the village encompasses not just families and churches but also government itself. She has spoken often of the government's obligations to universal health care, education, family leave, income supplements, and child care.

This divide between individual and social responsibility is a relatively recent phenomenon in our politics. The Bush emphasis on self-improvement and self-control was once intimately linked to the cause of social reform itself. Many of those who favored the prohibition of alcohol in the last century did not see it as an alternative to social reconstruction. On the contrary, it was a vital movement for social reconstruction that encompassed women's rights and economic independence, reform of trade agreements and governing structures, protection of local community values, as well as reform of individuals.

This link between self-improvement and social improvement was visible in the early trade union movement, which put heavy emphasis on education and self-help, even as it also preached organizing and solidarity. It was also powerful in the civil rights movement, and especially in the preaching of Martin Luther King Jr. In his moving book *Radical Equations: Math Literacy and Civil Rights* (coauthored by Charles E. Cobb Jr.), the legendary civil rights leader Robert Moses captured the magic of that moment. "The civil rights movement of the 1960s," he wrote, "was less about challenges and protests against white power than feeling our way toward our own power and possibilities — really a series of challenges by ourselves, and our communities, to ourselves." This was a movement that placed demands on society and on individuals.

To understand the current divisions in our religious traditions, it's essential to confront the new divide between those who stress personal conversion and those who seek social and economic transformation.

Two causes that were often allies in our nation's politics now often face off against each other as adversaries.

A few years ago, I was fortunate to edit a volume called *Lifting Up the Poor*, in which two of the nation's leading voices on welfare policy debated the religious underpinnings of their disagreements. In an especially thoughtful and searching way, they hit upon the essentials of so many of those back fence debates among religious believers.

Mary Jo Bane, a liberal Catholic and an assistant secretary of Health and Human Services in the Clinton administration, supported a strong government role in social provision. Her view was rooted in a sensibility she described as "hopeful rather than despairing, trusting rather than suspicious, more generous than prudent, more communitarian than individualistic." While acknowledging that the Scriptures "do not enlighten us much on the questions of who is obligated to provide what for whom under what conditions," she was unabashed in endorsing communal provision.

"My moral argument," she wrote, "asserts that the community is obligated to provide basic levels of subsistence, health care, and education to all its members. The obligation is based on the preciousness of every human being and on the belief that God's plan desires the flourishing of every person."

Lawrence M. Mead, a moderately conservative evangelical and a professor of politics at New York University, sees the gospel's call for salvation as restoring individuals to full moral agency. Economic poverty, as he sees is, is not the paramount concern of Christ's preaching. "There is no preference for the poor," he insists, "only a lively concern for them as well as other people in trouble. Jesus does help the needy and commands his followers to do so, but he has other concerns which are not economic, and he is not undemanding toward those he helps."

The key for Mead is to overcome a culture of poverty that he sees as a "defeatist culture." This culture has many effects. "Unwed pregnancy and drug addiction would appear to be self-defeating, irrational behaviors for those who adopt them," Mead writes. "The idea that people 'choose' these lifestyles attributes to them more power to control their lives than, inwardly, the seriously poor appear to have." Mead advocates an unashamedly "paternalistic" approach to the poor based on the idea that "if you receive some benefits, you accept some obligations in return."

Mead is not unconcerned about the poor and Bane is not unconcerned about personal responsibility. Yet note the difference in emphasis: Bane tends to emphasize the structural causes of poverty, Mead individual shortcomings rooted in a flawed culture.

This is the central divide among religious Americans over government's role in alleviating poverty (and a parallel analysis would find the same divide concerning public health, the environment, and disaster relief). It is a schism just as rooted in values as the more publicized debates over abortion and gay marriage. It has large implications for the poor. Progressives cannot ignore it, partly because more-conservative religious Americans who so often demonstrate abundant financial generosity toward the poor in their private lives ought to be the allies of their more moderate and liberal brothers and sisters in creating a more socially decent society.

What is required of progressives? The argument for personal responsibility cannot be ignored, and reforging the link between social and personal responsibility ought to be a battle cry of religious progressives. The poor suffer from high rates of teen pregnancy, fatherless families, and family breakup and they suffer from unjust social structures, large changes in the economy that produce greater inequality, and — in the case of African Americans and Latinos — racism. There is no reason for progressives to be silent about either half of that sentence, and no good reason for conservatives to deny the second half. By speaking out for personal responsibility, religious progressives can challenge their conservative friends to get serious about social responsibility.

But religious progressives also need to challenge the core conservative contention that government help for the less fortunate inevitably produces "dependency." Our nation moved closer to "equality of opportunity" because of extensive government efforts to offer individuals opportunities to develop their own capacities (and to offer minorities and women protection against discrimination). As legal philosopher Stephen Holmes has pointed out, Adam Smith, the intellectual father of the free market, favored a publicly financed, compulsory system of elementary education. After World War II the government's investment in the college education of millions through the GI Bill simultaneously opened new opportunities for individuals and promoted an explosive period of general economic growth. As

Holmes put it: "Far from being a road to serfdom, government intervention was meant to enhance individual autonomy. Publicly financed schooling, as [John Stuart] Mill wrote, is 'help toward doing without help.' "

Progressives also need to challenge a core conservative view that private and religious charity is sufficient to the task of alleviating poverty. That is simply not true. In an important 1997 article in *Commentary* magazine — hardly a bastion of liberalism — William Bennett and John DiIulio made the crucial calculations: "If all of America's grant-making private foundations gave away all of their income and all of their assets, they could cover only a year's worth of current government expenditures on social welfare." What would happen the next year?

They cited a study by Princeton's Julian Walpole of 125,000 charities, each with receipts of $25,000 a year or more. Among them, they raised and spent $350 billion annually. That sounds like a lot until you realize that this is only one-seventh of what is spent each year by federal, state, and local governments.

Bennett and DiIulio, neither of them enthusiasts of the old welfare state, concluded: "It is unlikely that Americans will donate much more than their present 2 percent of annual household income, or that corporate giving will take up any significant proportion of the slack in the event of future government reductions." The title of their article was "What Good Is Government?" Their answer was clear.

But religious progressives also need to engage in a dialogue with their conservative brothers and sisters on the most basic questions related to values and virtues. Religious conservatives and liberals share an aversion to excessive materialism. They agree that the market should not be the only arbiter of values. They agree that everything cannot and should not be bought and sold.

We do not, for example, believe that justice in the courts or votes and public offices should be bought and sold. We do not now (though many Americans once did) believe that human beings should be bought and sold. But these do not exhaust the instances in which free people might decide to limit the writ of money and the supremacy of the market. As political philosopher Michael Walzer has argued, one of the central issues confronting democratic societies concerns which rights and privileges should not be put up for sale.

As an abstract proposition, we reject the notion that a wealthy person should be able to buy extra years of life that a poor person cannot, since life itself ought not be bought and sold. Yet the availability of health care affects longevity, and by making health care a purely market transaction, we come close to selling life and death. This was the primary argument for Medicare and remains the central moral claim made by advocates of national health insurance. Similarly, we do not believe that children should be deprived of access to food, medicine, or education just because their parents are poor — or, for that matter, irresponsible. As Holmes said: "Why should children be hopelessly snared in a web of underprivilege into which they were born through no fault of their own?"

The relationship between the moral and economic crises in our society can be seen most powerfully in families where the need to earn enough income forces both parents to spend increasing amounts of time outside the home. One of the great achievements of the last century was "the family wage," which allowed the vast majority of workers to provide their families with both a decent living and the parental time to give their children a decent upbringing. The family wage was not simply a product of the marketplace. It was secured through a combination of economic growth, social legislation, and unionization. If the marketplace becomes not simply the main arbiter of income, as it will inevitably be, but the only judge of living standards, then all social factors, including the need to strengthen families and improve the care of children, become entirely irrelevant in the world of work.

The moral crisis so many conservatives talk about thus grows not simply from the "countercultural" or "permissive" ideas that developed in the 1960s. Its roots lie deeper, in a society that threatens to allow market values to crowd out all other values. The result is a steady erosion of the bonds of solidarity, morality, and trust. This affects the values put forward by the popular culture, the organization of family life, and the aspirations of the next generation — all questions of vital concern to religious conservatives.

My friend the late Father Philip Murnion regularly offered his friends in the Catholic social justice community a powerful insight from the time he spent as a child on welfare after his father died. In his day, Murnion said, poor children could count on three basic forms of support: some money from government, love and nurturing within the family, and moral guidance from churches and neighbors who lived in relatively safe and orderly communities. Now, he argued, poor children are under threat in all three spheres: Government help is in danger; many of the poorest children live in difficult (and at times dangerous) family situations; and the moral order and physical safety of many neighborhoods has collapsed.

Social justice requires economic support from government, a concern for family life, and serious efforts to strengthen community institutions and to restore public order. Religious progressives may find their vocation in insisting that our society needs to grapple with each of these issues. At the heart of their arguments should be two principles: Compassion is good, but justice is better. And while government certainly cannot solve all problems, what government does — and fails to do — still matters enormously.

E. J. Dionne Jr. was a syndicated columnist and senior fellow at The Brookings Institution in Washington, D.C., when this article appeared in Sojourners *magazine.*

What the Waters Revealed

BY JIM WALLIS

Hurricane Katrina destroyed entire cities, the lives of more than a thousand people, the homes of hundreds of thousands, and the confidence of millions in the government's commitment and ability to protect them. Then Hurricane Rita reflooded New Orleans and caused millions to flee their homes in Texas, including many who had already fled there from their homes in New Orleans. Much of New Orleans was emptied of its people, and broad areas of the Gulf Coast in Mississippi, Alabama, and Texas were devastated. More than one million Americans are now displaced across the country, and their fellow Americans around the nation are trying to take them in, perhaps for a long time.

But the waters of Hurricane Katrina also washed away our national denial of the shockingly high number of Americans living in poverty and our reluctance to admit the still-persistent connection of race and poverty in America, and perhaps even eroded the political power of a conservative anti-social services ideology that, for decades now, has weakened the idea of the common good.

The pictures from New Orleans stunned the nation. They exposed the stark reality of who was suffering the most, who was left behind, who was waiting in vain for help to arrive, and who is now facing the most difficult challenges of recovery. The faces of those stranded in New Orleans were overwhelmingly poor and black, the very old and the very young. They were the ones who could not evacuate; had no cars or money for gas; no money for bus, train, or airfare; no budget for hotels or no friends or family with room to share or spare. They were already vulnerable before this calamity; now they were totally exposed and on their own. For days, nobody came for them. And the conditions of the places they were finally herded to ("like animals," many testified) sickened the nation. Those left behind in New Orleans had already been left out in America.

From the reporters covering the unprecedented disaster to ordinary Americans glued to their televisions, a shocked and even outraged response was repeated: "I didn't realize how many Americans were poor."

"We have now seen what is under the rock in America," said a carpenter in Washington, D.C. The vulnerability of the poorest children in New Orleans has been especially riveting to many Americans, especially to other parents. Many say they had trouble holding back their tears when they saw mothers with their babies stranded on rooftops crying for help or jammed into dangerous and dirty places waiting for help to arrive.

As a direct result of Katrina and its aftermath, and for the first time in many years, the media were reporting on poverty, telling Americans that New Orleans had an overall poverty rate of 28 percent (84 percent of them African American), and a child poverty rate of almost 50 percent — half of all the city's children (rates only a little higher than other major cities and actually a little lower than some others). Ironically (and some might say providentially), the annual U.S. Census poverty report came out during Katrina's deadly assault, showing that poverty had risen for the fourth straight year and that 37 million Americans were stuck below the poverty line. Such people were the ones most stuck in New Orleans.

Katrina revealed what was already there in America: an invisible and often silent poverty that most of us in the richest nation on earth have chosen not to talk about, let alone take responsibility for. After the storm hit, we all saw it — and so did the rest of the world. It made Americans feel both compassion and shame. Many political leaders and commentators, across the ideological spectrum, acknowledged the national tragedy, not just of the horrendous storm but of the realities the flood waters exposed. And some have suggested that if the aftermath of Katrina finally leads the nation to demand solutions to the poverty of upwards of a third of its citizens, then something good might come from this terrible disaster.

That is what we must all work toward now. Rescuing those still in danger, assisting those in dire need, relocating and caring for the homeless, and beginning the process of recovery and rebuilding are all top priorities. But dealing with the stark and shameful social and racial realities Katrina has revealed must become our clear, long-term goal. That will require a combination of public and private initiatives, the merger of personal and social responsibility, the rebuilding of both families and communities — but also the confronting of hard questions about national priorities. Most of all it will require us to make different choices.

The critical needs of poor and low-income families must become the first priority of federal and state legislatures, not the last. And, the blatant inequalities of race in America — especially in critical areas of education, jobs, health care, and housing — must now be addressed. Congressional pork-barrel spending that aligns with political power more than human needs must be challenged as never before. That will require a complete reversal of the political logic now operating in Washington and state capitals around the country: A new moral logic must reshape our political habits.

In the face of this natural disaster — and during a time of war, with already rising deficits — new budget cuts to vital programs such as food stamps and Medicaid, and more tax cuts for the wealthy, in the form of estate tax repeal and capital gains and stock dividend reductions, would be both irresponsible and shameless.

The nation is starting to realize that the weakness of the nation's infrastructure is not a problem limited to the levees of New Orleans, and that restoring the Gulf Coast will require an environmental reconstruction as well. We can no longer neglect the loss of critical wetlands that once offered some protection from flooding, or deny the fact that increased water temperature in the Gulf of Mexico stokes the strength of tropical storms — such negligence is irresponsible and will only produce more disasters.

Katrina has also focused new attention on Iraq. The growing human and economic costs of a war in Iraq that more and more Americans believe to be a terrible mistake has also become an increasingly controversial issue as the current disaster has unfolded. Resources diverted from urgently needed levee repair in order to pay for war, the diminished availability of National Guard troops and first responders on tour in Iraq, and the embarrassing comparisons between poor planning and implementation for war and the ill-preparedness and incompetence of the national response to Katrina have all raised new and deeper questions about the nation's foreign policy and political leadership. A bad war, bad financial choices of how we spend our resources, and a bad strategy to combat terrorism are now inextricably linked in the minds of many to a bad natural disaster strategy, or lack thereof. The war in Iraq hasn't made us more secure; Katrina's aftermath has made that even more clear.

There is historical precedent for natural disasters provoking a reevaluation of our social thinking and political direction. In 1889, a great flood in Johnstown, Pennsylvania, trapped and killed hundreds of people, most of them poor. Some of the blame fell on the Pittsburgh millionaires whose private fishing pond overflowed onto the destitute. The tragic event helped to catalyze the already growing popular anger against the new industrialists who seemed so callous to the suffering of people around them. The flood, many historians feel, helped to prepare the way for the turn-of-the-century progressive movement, which focused on breaking up the powerful corporate trusts that had come to dominate the country.

In 1927, another flood visited destruction on the city of New Orleans. In his provocative book *Rising Tide: The Great Mississippi Flood of 1927 and How It Changed America*, historian John M. Barry describes how the disaster revealed both racial and economic inequalities. The response to the disaster by local authorities directly exposed the brutal inequities of race and class and provoked a deep populist anger. People demanded new responses from the federal government, and the 1927 flood helped pave the way for the New Deal. Citing both Johnstown and 1927 New Orleans as examples, columnist David Brooks wrote insightfully in the *New York Times* immediately following Katrina, "Hurricanes come in two waves. First comes the rainstorm, and then comes what the historian John Barry calls the 'human storm' — the recriminations, the political conflict, and the battle over compensation. Floods wash away the surface of society, the settled way things have been done. They expose the underlying power structures, the injustices, the patterns of corruption, and the unacknowledged inequalities. When you look back over the meteorological turbulence in this nation's history, it's striking how often political turbulence followed." Such natural disasters, says Brooks, can become "civic examinations."

Interviewing Barry on *Meet the Press*, Tim Russert asked, "Do you see the same thing happening now in terms of the reemergence of class and race and poverty as political issues?" Barry replied, "I think it's certainly possible and maybe likely. But it's obviously too early to tell." The storm "ripped off the cover" from America, said Barry, revealing what happens to people without resources. The question, said the historian, is whether Katrina would cause a "shift in public thinking" about our collective responsibilities to people in need.

That shift in thinking cannot just be the reassertion of old social and political agendas that seek to take advantage of the current moment of opportunity. The truth is that our failure of the poor is a collective one: Both conservative and liberal agendas have proven inadequate and left us with a very large underclass of poor people — adults, children, families — in America. Both sides have important insights that must be factored into any real solutions, but both have fallen far short of providing real answers. Many, even most, poor people work hard, full time, yet are still forced to raise their children in poverty. That should be unacceptable in America. To change that, we will need a new commitment, a new approach, and a new alliance to overcome poverty in America.

There are two obstacles to making real progress against poverty: the lack of priority and the lack of agreement on strategy. The poor have been near the bottom of our priority list, if they are on the list at all. It will take a moral and even religious imperative to change our priorities, but the time has come to do so. But we have also been paralyzed by the debate between liberals and conservatives on what solutions to pursue, with the Right favoring cultural changes and the Left endorsing policy changes.

We must be disciplined by results when it comes to poverty reduction. It's time to move from the politics of blame to a politics of solutions. Liberals must start talking about the problems of out-of-wedlock births and about strengthening both marriage and parenting, and conservatives must start talking about strategic public investments in education, health care, affordable housing, and living family incomes. We must focus on making work really work for low-income families. Those who work hard and full time in America should not have to raise their children in poverty — but many still do. Together, we must end the debate that's limited to the choices of large or small government and forge a common commitment to good and effective government.

This is indeed a teachable moment, but one that will require good teachers. What have we learned, how must we change, where will we transform our priorities, and when will we commit ourselves to forging a new strategy that actually might work to defeat the cycle of poverty?

Restoring the hope of America's poorest families, renewing our national infrastructures, protecting our environmental stability, and rethinking our most basic priorities will require nothing less than a national change of heart and direction. It calls for a transformation of political ethics and governance, a move from serving private interests to ensuring the public good. If Katrina changes our political conscience and reinvigorates among us a commitment to the common good, then even this terrible tragedy might be redeemed.

Jim Wallis is editor-in-chief of Sojourners *magazine. This article appeared in the November 2005 issue of* Sojourners.

India on 20 Cents a Day

BY ASEEM SHRIVASTAVA

The World Bank started making international comparisons of poverty only about two decades back. For obvious reasons of convenience, it developed two simple notions of poverty. The lower poverty line was set at $1 a day per capita. Those below it were considered to be "the poorest of the poor." The upper poverty line was set at $2 a day. Those living on $1 to 2 a day were still poor, but not as bad off.

However, there was a problem. It was realized that $1 goes much farther in purchasing necessary items of consumption in a poor country than in a rich one. To make purchasing power across countries comparable, economists developed what is known as the PPP (purchasing power parity) index. Taking into account the lower cost of living in impoverished countries, a conversion factor is now applied to market exchange rates to calculate what is minimally necessary to survive there. Using World Bank numbers, applying this conversion factor for India effectively means that if you survive on 1 PPP dollar a day in that country, it is equivalent to being given 20 cents in your hand in the U.S.

A dominant impression is that the poor are living on less than $1 a day. In fact, it would be enormously more accurate, as far as everyday English is concerned, to say that the poor across the world are living on less than 20 cents a day. The reason why this is not done is obvious: It would give an even-more-alarming picture of the scale and depth of poverty across this enormously wealthy world. Most decent people are shocked enough by the understated numbers in the form they are widely quoted. More reality would numb and paralyze even the grittiest of activists. "Humanity," T. S. Eliot wrote, "cannot bear much reality." He had the privileged in mind.

The most recent World Bank estimates for India are based on household surveys carried out in 1999–2000. It was found that almost 80 percent of India's population was surviving on less than $2.15 a day (in PPP terms). That is, about 800 million people were living on 40 cents a day or less. Nearly 35 percent (350 million) were found to be living on 20 cents a day or less. Thanks to the subtleties of PPP calculations, it may quite possibly be the case that the number of people across the world who are not able to meet the minimum standards for adequate nutrition is anywhere from 3 to 4 billion, rather than the officially estimated 2.7 billion who are estimated to be living under $2 a day. No one really knows. In other words, we could be off by a whole continent!

In our increasingly packaged consumerist world, even global poverty figures must ultimately arrive in a wrapping that is not unpalatably unattractive to the public. Trickle-down will ultimately work, we are repeatedly assured by growth economists. But faith in trickle-down, as John Kenneth Galbraith is said to have remarked, is a bit like feeding race horses superior oats so that starving sparrows can forage in their dung. All indications, especially in parts of the world like rural India, are that a decade and a half of corporate globalization has left under nutrition and malnutrition all but intact and might quite possibly have worsened the predicament for many millions.

Perhaps we would do well to remember Einstein's counsel: "Everything that can be counted does not necessarily count; everything that counts cannot necessarily be counted." We only count and measure what is useful, important, or interesting to us. By using a severely distorted measure like a poverty line pegged unreasonably low, public authorities and governments reveal that they don't care nearly as much about poverty as they do, for instance, about the growth rate or the stock market index. The poverty measurement industry loses much sleep and sweat over details that do not matter much. The big picture, perhaps unsurprisingly, is inaccurately reported.

If global poverty statistics are not disseminated accurately, the facts on the ground will only get worse — thanks to misinformed policy making, among other things. And the potential consequences across the globe could be nothing short of catastrophic.

Aseem Shrivastava was an independent writer when this article appeared in the February 2007 issue of Sojourners *magazine.*

The Roots of Justice Revival

BY JIM RICE

When Charles Finney preached, people listened. Finney, considered one of America's greatest evangelists of the nineteenth century and a leader of what later become known as the "Second Great Awakening," drew enthusiastic crowds at his revival services.

A contemporary of Finney's, Rev. Charles P. Bush, described the scene at one of his revivals: "The churches were not large enough to hold the multitudes that thronged to hear him. After the pews were all filled, the aisles and areas would be supplied with chairs and benches; persons would sit as close as possible all over the pulpit stairs; and still others, men and women, and children, would stand wherever standing-room could be found, throughout a long and exhausting service."

Finney's preaching had a lasting effect, not only on the personal lives of those who heard him but also on the broader society. In his memoirs, Finney himself described the impact of one of his revivals: "This revival made a great change in the moral state and subsequent history of Rochester. The great majority of the leading men and women in the city were converted.... From night to night I had been making appeals to the congregation, and calling forward those that were prepared to give their hearts to God; and large numbers were converted every evening."

Finney, who believed strongly that salvation came through grace alone by faith, saw "works" — the way people act in the world, including, in his case, adamant opposition to the abomination of slavery — as evidence of faith. He wrote, "When I first went to New York, I had made up my mind on the question of slavery, and was exceedingly anxious to arouse public attention to the subject ... in my prayers and preaching, I so often alluded to slavery, and denounced it, that a considerable excitement came to exist among the people."

He later commented that acceptance of slavery in the South seemed to block the religious awakening that was happening elsewhere. "A divine influence seemed to pervade the whole land," Finney wrote. "Slavery seemed to shut it out from the South. The people there were in such a state of irritation, of vexation, and of committal to their peculiar institution, which had come to be assailed on every side, that the Spirit of God seemed to be grieved away from them. There seemed to be no place found for him in the hearts of the Southern people at that time."

Finney, of course, wasn't alone in linking revival to social reform. Jonathan Blanchard was the founder of Wheaton College and another leader of nineteenth-century evangelism. In his 1839 commencement address at Oberlin College, which he titled "A Perfect State of Society," Blanchard affirmed that "every true minister of Christ is a universal reformer, whose business it is, so far as possible, to reform all the evils which press on human concerns." For Blanchard, being a "minister of Christ" meant, in today's terms, becoming an activist on behalf of social justice.

When critics of the day argued that Christians ought not to be focused on this world, Blanchard responded that while "the kingdom is not of this world, it is in it." Blanchard's evangelical approach to social reform understood the balance: On the one hand, imperfect human beings cannot, through their own power, bring about the kingdom of God on earth — that would constitute "works righteousness," a reliance on something other than God's grace. But at the same time, Christians are called to "reform all the evils" in the world, as Blanchard put it.

Blanchard approached the question of social reform — and specifically the abolition of slavery — in theological terms. He wrote, "Slave-holding is in itself sinful and the relationship between master and slave a sinful relationship." It was not, in Blanchard's view, merely a violation of human rights, or a crime — it was a sin. The abolition of slavery became a matter of faith for these followers of Jesus.

Finney, like Blanchard, did not conflate "revival" and "reform" into one; he didn't stop calling people to conversion. Rather, he saw social reforms — such as temperance and the abolition of slavery — as "appendages" of revival, the fruits of conversion. Finney's use of the term "appendage" did not imply that he thought the reforms he was involved in were unimportant — in fact, he devoted much of his life to these reform movements. Rather, the metaphor emphasized that the "heart" of evangelism was conversion to Jesus, with the natural outgrowth of reform being like a person's arms or legs — appendages, yes, but certainly significant to a person's existence, and neither discretionary nor expendable.

For Finney, involvement in reform efforts was not optional, and the lack of such involvement hampered the revival movement. In his "Lectures on Revivals of Religion," Finney wrote, "Revivals are hindered when ministers and churches take wrong ground in regard to any question involving human rights." Note his emphasis: It was the revivals that were hindered when believers failed to act on behalf of human rights. In fact, Finney felt that the spiritual vitality of a church was sapped by a failure to embrace reform. When the church fails to speak out on such issues, Finney wrote, "She is perjured, and the Spirit of God departs from her." Commitment to the reform of society was seen by Finney as a spiritual issue, a sign of holiness, and not just a matter of "secular" politics.

Finney, who has been called the "father of modern revivalism," called for revival as a means of "breaking the power of the world and of sin over Christians." The essence of sin was selfishness, Finney taught, and to be converted from sin meant to turn from selfishness toward benevolence, doing good to all and becoming "useful" in the world. The key vehicles for these actions included hundreds of "benevolent societies" that focused on every imaginable social evil, from alcohol and slavery to the mistreatment of women. He could even be considered an early feminist, in that — in the face of criticism — he invited women to speak publicly at his revivals. Finney served as president of Oberlin, which became the first college in the country to award bachelor's degrees to women and African Americans, and which was a stop on the "underground railroad" for escaping slaves.

Other nineteenth-century evangelists similarly connected Christian conversion with social reform. A prominent example was Henry Ward Beecher, whom historian William G. McLoughlin called "unquestionably the outstanding popular spokesman of evangelical religion in nineteenth-century America," as well as a "model for evangelical preachers of his day across the nation." Beecher argued that for Christian preaching to be legitimate, it must address the issues of the day — and disturb the status quo: "That [person] who so preaches Christ, doctrinally or historically, that no one takes offense, no one feels rebuked, no one trembles, is not a legitimate and faithful preacher of Christ."

Beecher was clear in the conviction that the central focus of Christian preaching was always "Jesus Christ, and him crucified" (1 Corinthians 2:2). But Beecher didn't stop there. He went on to address "all reformations of evil in society" — in other words, questions of social justice — which in Beecher's view must spring from the "vital center" of "preaching Christ." Addressing social evils, however, was not optional for the Christian: It would be a "dangerous thing," he wrote, to preach in a way that was not a constant rebuke to "all the evil in the community."

Many of the other leaders of the most important U.S. social justice movements of the nineteenth century were also evangelical Christians. Along with Blanchard, Finney, and Beecher, other Christians were deeply involved not only in the abolition movement, but also in reform efforts regarding temperance, the role of women, peacemaking, and many other issues of the day. Today's movements for human rights and social justice are very much rooted in this evangelical revivalist tradition, a fact that is too little acknowledged by many who are successors to this legacy.

The false dichotomy of recent decades — that one kind of Christian talks about "evangelism" and "revival" and another kind altogether focuses on justice — is beginning to crack. Many Christians today have rediscovered the heritage of the nineteenth-century revivalist reformers. Many Christians — from all strands of the church, mainline and evangelical, Protestant and Catholic — have come to understand that working for social justice is a constitutive aspect of the gospel and that "withdrawal" from the world is not an option. They have come to see, as Finney put it, "The Christian church has it in her power to reform this nation.... No [nation] has had strength to resist any reform which God's people have unitedly demanded."

Jim Rice is editor of Sojourners *magazine. This article appeared in the April 2008 issue of* Sojourners.

Where do Christians turn for a faithful perspective on news and culture?

sojourners
Faith in Action for Social Justice

[] Yes! Send me a free trial issue of *Sojourners* magazine.

If I like it, I'll pay just $29.95 for a one-year subscription—a savings of $10. If *Sojourners* isn't for me, I'll return the invoice marked "cancel," and the first issue is free for me to keep.

Name _____

Address _____

City _____

State/Zip _____

E-mail _____
S1004ZJP

Offer good for U.S. addresses only. Look for your trial issue to arrive within four to six weeks!

Mail to: Sojourners Magazine
P.O. Box 48
Congers, NY 10920-9857

Learn more at www.sojo.net

Share Your Thoughts

With the Author: Your comments will be forwarded to the author when you send them to *zauthor@zondervan.com*.

With Zondervan: Submit your review of this book by writing to *zreview@zondervan.com*.

Free Online Resources at

www.zondervan.com

Zondervan AuthorTracker: Be notified whenever your favorite authors publish new books, go on tour, or post an update about what's happening in their lives at www.zondervan.com/authortracker.

Daily Bible Verses and Devotions: Enrich your life with daily Bible verses or devotions that help you start every morning focused on God. Visit www.zondervan.com/newsletters.

Free Email Publications: Sign up for newsletters on Christian living, academic resources, church ministry, fiction, children's resources, and more. Visit www.zondervan.com/newsletters.

Zondervan Bible Search: Find and compare Bible passages in a variety of translations at www.zondervanbiblesearch.com.

Other Benefits: Register yourself to receive online benefits like coupons and special offers, or to participate in research.

■ ZONDERVAN®

ZONDERVAN.com/
AUTHOR**TRACKER**
follow your favorite authors